MEAL PREP

THE AUSTRALIAN

Women's Weekly

MEAL
PREP

THE AUSTRALIAN WOMEN'S WEEKLY TEST KITCHEN

TRIPLE TESTED

CONTENTS

MEAL PREP IT FORWARD

WE'VE ALL BEEN THERE. YOU'VE RUSHED HOME FROM THE OFFICE, MISSED THE SUPERMARKET ALONG THE WAY AND HAVE NO IDEA WHAT'S FOR DINNER. THE FRIDGE IS LOOKING SPARSE, EVERYONE'S HUNGRY, AND INSPIRATION, LET ALONE INGREDIENTS, HAS GONE RESOLUTELY AWOL. WE MAY HAVE THE BEST INTENTIONS TO COOK NUTRITIOUS, HOMEMADE DINNERS EVERY NIGHT, BUT THE REALITY OF ROUTINELY MAKING MEALS FROM SCRATCH IS CHALLENGING. TIME PRESSURES FROM WORK, FAMILY AND LIFE IN GENERAL CAN CONSPIRE TO MAKE MEAL PREP SEEM AN IMPOSSIBLE TASK – OR, AT THE VERY LEAST, ONE THAT'S NOT EXACTLY ENJOYABLE. WHEN FRESH IDEAS AND MOTIVATION DRAIN AWAY, IT'S EASY TO SETTLE FOR TAKEAWAY OR CONVENIENCE FOOD, WHICH IS NEITHER SATISFYING NOR SUSTAINABLE IN THE LONG TERM. SO IF YOU'RE IN A MEAL-PLANNING RUT AND SEARCHING FOR NEW WAYS TO GET OUT OF THAT NIGHTLY WHAT-TO-COOK CONUNDRUM, THIS BOOK IS EXACTLY WHAT YOU NEED.

Each recipe then spins off into four simple, quickly prepared variations: by mastering one recipe, you instantly have four others in your repertoire so you can mix things up a little. The idea is that you cook a base recipe, portion and refrigerate (or freeze) it, then utilise this prepped food for meals during the week. Of course, you can simply cook and eat a recipe without storing it (the whole base recipe serves four), but the concept here is as much about flexibility as it is about providing home-made, interesting and healthy meals throughout the week. For the time it takes to prepare a single dinner for four, it takes relatively little extra time in the kitchen to bulk-cook and whip up two, three or even four different dinners, then portion these into containers to make into convenient and delicious meals to have on hand when needed. By setting aside some time on the weekend (such as Sunday afternoon) for meal prep, you'll save time and stress during your working week.

As well as the Pick Your Protein recipes with their four-way spin-offs, we've included a chapter filled with clever recipes designed to freeze and reheat. When looking for time efficiencies, the freezer is every cook's best friend; you'll be amazed at what you can freeze. Roast Chicken with Green Pumpkin and Broccolini Curry... Mushroom and Kale Lasagne... Moroccan Pulled Beef... There are even fish recipes that will happily freeze and reheat.

All the recipes in this book tap into a modern, cosmopolitan vibe, so there's no risk of flavour fatigue. For example, Hoisin Beef with 'Quickled' Cucumbers morphs into No Carb Pho one day, Chilli Beef Noodles the next and finally a Mushu Beef Wrap. Chilli Glazed Salmon with Kimchi Corn becomes Korean Salmon Zoodle Bowl, Kimchi Salmon Tacos and Korean Beans and Egg Bowl. Every ingredient you need for the spin-off dishes are listed within the structure of each main recipe, so you can see at a glance all that you'll require. You might find you prefer one spin-off over another, and the great thing about this mix-and-match approach is that it's flexible; use the recipes in ways that suit you best.

Did we mention there are also some breakfast recipes? Many people skip this important meal due to lack of time or not having the right ingredients on hand. Or they eat convenience breakfast foods of dubious nutritional value. But with good planning and kitchen management, even the busiest people can make healthy, delicious, made-from-scratch breakfasts, every single day.

BY SETTING ASIDE SOME TIME ON THE WEEKEND (SUCH AS SUNDAY AFTERNOON) FOR MEAL PREP, YOU'LL SAVE TIME AND STRESS DURING YOUR WORKING WEEK.

PREP IT

IF YOU KNOW NOTHING ELSE ABOUT HOW PROFESSIONAL COOKS WORK, YOU'LL AT LEAST KNOW THIS – IT'S ALL ABOUT THE PREP. CHEFS GET THEIR 'MIS-EN-PLACE' (LITERALLY MEANING 'EVERYTHING IN ITS PLACE') DONE BEFORE THEY WARM AN OVEN OR HEAT A PAN. THE WAY THEY WORK IN PREPARING RAW MATERIALS FIRST, AND NOT AS THEY COOK, IS STREAMLINED TO MINIMISE WASTE AND MESS. THINK OF IT LIKE A PRODUCTION LINE. WITH PLANNING AND CARE, YOU TOO CAN SMARTEN YOUR MEAL PREP, MAKING IT BOTH TIME AND COST EFFICIENT. HERE ARE SOME TIPS FOR ACHIEVING THAT, AND GETTING THE MOST FROM THIS BOOK.

LISTS, LISTS, LISTS

Taking the time to write comprehensive shopping and to-do lists keeps planning and cooking efficient. Start by choosing the recipes you want to cook for the coming week. From there, appraise your pantry items and note anything extra you might need, then list types and amounts of meats, produce and other fresh ingredients required. Shop up to two days ahead for fresh foods. Ordering online and having them delivered further saves time, but remember you might want to appraise fruits and vegetables yourself for quality and freshness before you purchase, so shopping online for these items might not be ideal. Having detailed shopping lists ensures you won't buy anything you don't need, and avoid shopping when hungry as this can lead to poor purchasing decisions. If you have perishables in your fridge or freezer, plan meals around these first, to minimise waste.

SEASONALITY

Cooking for the season means buying fruit and vegetables when they are plentiful and cheaper, and also at their best. Some, such as tomatoes and stone fruits, lend themselves to being bulk-frozen raw for convenient use throughout the year.

> **BULK-PREPARE SPECIFIC INGREDIENTS TO CUT DOWN ON WEEKNIGHT COOKING TIMES: WASH, CHOP, SLICE OR MARINATE FRESH PRODUCE SO COMPONENTS OF A RECIPE ARE READY TO GO.**

EQUIPMENT

Make sure your equipment is up to scratch. Blunt knives make slow work of bulk chopping and slicing, and the extra force required to use them invites cutting accidents. Invest in sturdy chopping boards, reserving one for raw meat preparation to avoid cross-contamination, and a small one just for garlic, which can taint boards. Have plenty of stainless steel bowls in a variety of sizes, a good-quality grater and ergonomic vegetable peelers, and a range of larger saucepans, casserole dishes and frying pans if you plan to cook multiples of recipes. A food processor is indispensable for speeding up certain types of prep, and a stick blender, with a small processor attachment, is worth its weight in gold, too.

READY, PREP, COOK

You needn't write off your entire Sunday to prep for the week; there are a few different strategies to employ:

1 Fill the freezer with family meals to reheat during the week and beyond. By bulk-cooking three or four recipes, you'll have a variety of meals for a few weeks. Note that freezable meals in this book will keep for 2–6 months in the freezer (see our fridge & freezer guide on page 17 for more information on freezing times).

2 Pre-cook individual meals for reheating, a handy approach if members of your household come home at different times each night. Freezing smaller portions means quicker reheating.

3 Bulk-prepare specific ingredients to cut down on weeknight cooking times: chop, slice or marinate fresh produce so components of a recipe are ready to go. For example, prepare (peel, cut etc.) dry firm vegetables that don't discolour, such as cauliflower, broccoli or carrots, up to 5 days in advance and store them in the fridge in resealable plastic bags or containers. Only wash chopped produce just before you cook it, as water can cause dampness, encouraging mould to grow. You can peel and chop onion and freeze it in resealable plastic bags until required.

4 Remember to enlist help! Get your partner, children or entire family into the kitchen to assist with food prep. Note that many of the base recipes in this book take only 25–35 minutes to prepare and cook.

FRIDGE BASICS

KEEP STOCKED UP ON THESE SUGGESTIONS FOR SAUCES, CONDIMENTS, PICKLES AND PRESERVES TO BUILD FLAVOUR IN YOUR MEALS. THESE WILL TAKE UP LESS ROOM IN THE FRIDGE, ALLOWING MORE ROOM FOR PERISHABLE FOODS.

1

SAUCES & CONDIMENTS

Chilli sauces, miso (white and red), red curry paste, tahini, soy sauces, indian spice pastes and mustards are the basis for marinades and curries.

2

PICKLES & PRESERVES

Ingredients preserved in salt, brine, vinegar and oil, such as black and green olives, capers, kimchi, sauerkraut and preserved lemons, add interest in both flavour and texture.

3

CITRUS

Lemons, limes, oranges and mandarins can all be used for their rind, flesh and juice to add freshness. Kaffir lime leaves give a fragrant touch.

4

VEGETABLES

Celery, fennel, carrots, chillies and alliums, such as leeks, are the ideal flavour-base for casseroles and stews.

5

HERBS & AROMATICS

Buy ginger and lemongrass, and woody herbs like rosemary and thyme for longevity.

PANTRY BASICS

KEEPING THESE IN YOUR PANTRY MEANS YOU HAVE THE FLAVOUR-BOOSTING BASIS FOR MANY OF THESE MEAL PREP RECIPES, WITH ONLY A FEW EXTRA INGREDIENTS NEEDED TO TRANSFORM THESE STAPLES INTO DELICIOUS, SATISFYING MEALS.

1 VINEGARS & OILS

Whether you have two or 10 different oils and vinegars in your pantry, they add flavour to your cooking.

2 SPICES & SEASONINGS

Add spices and spice mixes to breathe life into savoury and sweet recipes, for flavour, colour and complexity.

3 GRAINS, NOODLES & PASTA

Wheat and egg pastas in myriad shapes. Coloured rices and ready-cooked sachets. Dried beans, lentils, quinoa and barley are protein rich.

4 CANNED FOODS

Must-haves are canned tomatoes, beans, lentils, and coconut milk and cream, all of which will form the base for so many dishes.

5 NUTS & SEEDS

Nutrient-dense, these are great for adding texture as well as flavour. Freeze in bags for long-term storage.

FOOD SAFETY

The biggest concern with a packed lunch is food safety. If it's not stored properly for the few hours before you eat it, bacteria can grow. Meat and dairy products are particularly prone. Other high-risk foods include fish, poultry, eggs and anything packaged in a jar or can, which can become high risk once opened. This is especially the case concerning children, as little ones can be more susceptible to food poisoning. Keeping foods cool is the key to food safety. If you don't have a lunch box that can be chilled, consider throwing a frozen ice-pack in with your packed box to keep food as cool as possible. Freezing a plastic bottle of water or juice will perform the same function and makes for a refreshingly chilled drink by the time lunchtime comes around too. Even using frozen bread slices for making sandwiches, and packing baked goods straight from the freezer, will keep things chilled for just that extra bit longer. The lowest risk foods for spoilage include uncooked fruits and vegetables, dried foods (crackers, biscuits and other baked goods) and pre-packaged foods such as popcorn, cereal bars and dried fruits.

PANTRY

Have a good pantry maintenance system in place to avoid waste; clean out the pantry regularly. Group items together in categories – oils, condiments, cereals, flours, dried fruits – and make sure you can easily see what's there so you don't double-buy. Write use-by dates on each jar label and keep a pad and paper (or blackboard) permanently handy so you can list items requiring restocking when you think of them. Institute a similar regime for your fridge too.

FRIDGE

Proper fridge management helps your food last longer. The general rules are: keep dairy products near the back of the fridge, not in the fridge door, as it's cooler there and they will keep longer. Store fruits and vegetables in the crisper section. Avocados, tomatoes, potatoes, onions, citrus, pears and bananas should be stored in a cool, dark cupboard, not the fridge; keep onions and potatoes separate as the gases they emit can cause produce next to them to spoil faster. Keep fresh meat on the lower shelf, on a tray to catch any juices that might leak out and to avoid cross-contamination.

SPEAKING OF PLASTIC

While we are all trying to move away from relying on it, plastic resealable bags make brilliant storage containers, extending the life of ultra-perishable, delicate items stored in the fridge, such as fresh herbs, lettuces and pre-prepared vegetables. Make sure to expel as much air as possible from the bag before sealing, and reuse the bag, if you can.

FREEZER

The freezer is your best friend when cooking ahead. Most things will freeze well, including soups, most sauces, casseroles, meatballs, muffins, pies and breads. Some things that don't freeze well are uncooked root vegetables, mayonnaise, crisp vegetables with a high water content such as cucumber and radish, and delicate, leafy vegetables like lettuce.

Remember, you can freeze certain cooked grains and legumes – cooked and cooled brown rice, quinoa and brown lentils will freeze for weeks in airtight containers. They can also be pre-cooked, refrigerated and re-heated, but in this scenario they should be consumed within 3 days.

It's important to cool all hot food to room temperature before refrigerating or freezing, to prevent harmful bacteria occurring. Putting hot foods in the fridge, especially soups and sauces, actually extends the time they remain in the temperature 'danger zone' for bacteria formation. When freezing, make sure containers are very full so there is minimal air; air gaps can cause water crystals and freezer burn to build up over time, affecting flavour and appearance.

The safest way to thaw anything is slowly and in the refrigerator. Remove items from the freezer to the fridge in the morning and thaw during the day. Leaving food on the bench to thaw can encourage pathogens to grow.

IT'S IMPORTANT TO COOL ALL HOT FOOD TO ROOM TEMPERATURE BEFORE REFRIGERATING OR FREEZING, TO PREVENT HARMFUL BACTERIA OCCURRING.

TYPES OF LUNCH BOXES

Lunch boxes come in many different styles and sizes, and in a range of materials, from plastic and nylon to stainless steel. It's important to have the right kind of box to protect your food and keep it safely at the right temperature until you eat it. What you pack your lunch in is as important as the lunch itself. Squashed sandwiches, leaked salad juices and crushed bananas are depressing scenarios and easily avoided by using a sturdy box. Have a variety of shapes and styles of lunch containers on hand to accommodate different seasons and types of lunches – one size doesn't fit all.

CLASSIC BOXES

A good lunch box is not only best for transporting food but is healthy for the environment as well. While a plastic bag may seem an easier option, it's more eco-friendly to use a box that will last for, in many instances, years. Boxes run the gamut of simple, economical supermarket buys to smart canvas bag-like boxes with multiple compartments. What works in summer may not work in winter; for example, boxes with a little ventilation are important for warmer ambient temperatures, as food more readily overheats and sweats when tightly enclosed.

BENTO BOXES

Boxes with different compartments are excellent when you need to separate your salad from your dips and your cheese from your chocolate cake. With this type of box there is no need to wrap foods, meaning less plastic, which in turn is better for the environment. Stainless steel is a great material as it is sturdy and washes well, without retaining food odours as plastic can.

THERMOS

Invest in a thermos flask to hold food at the right temperature for hours. For example, it will keep soups, casseroles and baked beans hot, and yoghurt, chilled soups and desserts safely cold for up to 6 hours. Some have two or more stackable compartments, cleverly designed for transporting both hot and chilled dishes at the same time. There are also freezable poly-canvas lunch bags with water-resistant lining, which you freeze overnight. These keep foods fresh for hours, without the hassle of including a separate ice-pack.

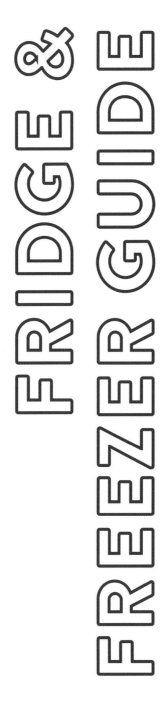

FRIDGE & FREEZER GUIDE

FOOD	FRIDGE	FREEZER
cured meats (whole salami/chorizo/bacon)	2 weeks	2 months
deli meats sliced to order (ham/turkey)	4–5 days	1–2 months
prepacked deli meats (unopened)	1 week (opened) 2 weeks (unopened)	1–2 months
cooked chicken dishes	3–4 days	4 months
cooked meat dishes	3–4 days	2–3 months
cooked fish dishes	3–4 days	4 months
soups & stews	3–4 days	2–3 months
hard cheeses (parmesan)	1–3 months	6 months
soft cheeses (ricotta)	10 days	not suitable
hard-boiled eggs	1 week	not suitable
cooked rice	3 days	4 months (reheat from frozen)
cooked vegies	3–4 days	2 months

This chart will help you determine how long you can store prepped meals in the fridge, as well as how long they can be frozen. Your fridge temperature should be at 5°C or below and the temperature of your freezer -15°C. Always store raw food and cooked food separately, in clean airtight containers. Meat, poultry and fish, and even rice must be refrigerated as soon as possible after cooking. This is especially important for casserole-type dishes; stand them for no longer than 1 hour to cool before transferring to the fridge or freezer. It is better to decant large quantities to smaller containers for rapid cooling. Modern fridges can cope with hot foods being placed in them. Items to be thawed must be thawed in the fridge, not left out on a bench. It is equally important when reheating food that it is reheated sufficiently and consumed immediately. Ensure food that is reheated in the microwave is stirred periodically. Thawed foods should never be refrozen.

WEEKLY MEAL PLANNER

	BREAKFAST	SNACK	LUNCH	SNACK	DINNER
M					
T					
W					
Th					
F					
S					
Su					

SHOPPING LIST

PANTRY

- ○
- ○
- ○
- ○
- ○
- ○
- ○
- ○
- ○
- ○
- ○
- ○
- ○
- ○
- ○
- ○
- ○
- ○
- ○
- ○

FRIDGE

- ○
- ○
- ○
- ○
- ○
- ○
- ○
- ○
- ○
- ○
- ○
- ○
- ○
- ○
- ○
- ○
- ○
- ○
- ○
- ○

FRUIT & VEG

- ○
- ○
- ○
- ○
- ○
- ○
- ○
- ○
- ○
- ○
- ○
- ○
- ○
- ○
- ○
- ○
- ○
- ○
- ○
- ○

GRAB + GO

BREAKFASTS

OVERNIGHT SEED BIRCHER

PREP TIME 15 MINUTES
(+ REFRIGERATION)
MAKES 4 PORTIONS

Combine 2 cups preferred
milk + 1 cup rolled oats
+ ½ cup pure apple juice
+ ⅓ cup each pepitas
(pumpkin seed kernels)
+ sunflower seeds + ¼ cup
ground linseeds (flaxseeds)
+ 1 tbsp each chia seeds
+ pure maple syrup. Cover;
refrigerate overnight. Serve
with fruit (see variations, right).

Meal 1 (see picture, far left) Cut ½ small red apple into julienne; combine with 1 tsp lemon juice. Serve 1 portion bircher (recipe, left) with apple mixture + 1 tbsp dried unsweetened cranberries + ¼ cup cherries + ½ small banana.

Meal 2 Serve 1 portion bircher (recipe, left) with ¼ small chopped papaya + ¼ cup sliced pineapple + 1 halved passionfruit.

Meal 3 Serve 1 portion bircher (recipe, left) with 1 diced peeled small peach + 4 quartered strawberries + ¼ cup raspberries.

Meal 4 Serve 1 portion bircher (recipe, left) with 1 chopped yellow or green kiwifruit + ½ each small sliced green apple + pear.

Tip The overnight seed bircher can be refrigerated for up to 4 days.

CHIA PUDDING WITH JAM SWIRL

PREP & COOK TIME
10 MINUTES (+ STANDING)
MAKES 4 PORTIONS

BERRY JAM Thaw 450g
(14½oz) frozen mixed berries;
stir thawed berries + ¼ cup
pure maple syrup in a pan
over medium heat for
10 minutes until jam-like.
Cool.

CHIA PUDDING Mix 1½ cups
coconut yoghurt + 1¾ cups
soy milk + ½ cup chia seeds
in a bowl until combined;
stand 10 minutes to thicken.

Meal 1 (see picture, far left) Top 1 portion chia pudding (recipe, left) with 1 portion berry jam (recipe, left) in a 1-cup container.

Meal 2 Swirl 1 portion berry jam (recipe, left) + 1 portion chia pudding (recipe, left) in a 1-cup container. Add 1 tbsp pure maple syrup + 1 tbsp chopped pistachios.

Meal 3 Swirl 1 portion berry jam (recipe, left) + 1 portion chia pudding (recipe, left) in a 1-cup container. Add 1½ tbsp peanut butter + ½ sliced small banana.

Meal 4 Swirl 1 portion berry jam (recipe, left) + 1 portion chia pudding (recipe, left) in a 1-cup container. Add 2 tbsp toasted natural seed mix + ½ medium green apple cut into matchsticks.

BEAN BURRITO BREKKY BOWLS

PREP & COOK TIME
10 MINUTES
MAKES 4 PORTIONS

BURRITO BEANS Combine a 400g (12½oz) can drained, rinsed four-bean mix + 2 tbsp chopped chipotle in adobo sauce + 35g (1oz) sachet burrito seasoning mix + ¾ cup chopped drained roasted capsicum.

Meal 1 (see picture, far left) Line a bowl with 1 jumbo tortilla. Add 1 portion burrito beans (recipe, left) + 1 cup baby spinach + ¼ sliced small red onion + 2 tbsp coriander (cilantro) leaves.

Meal 2 Heat 2 tsp olive oil in a pan over medium heat. Cook 1 egg whisked with 2 tbsp sour cream until scrambled. Line a bowl with 1 jumbo tortilla. Add 1 portion burrito beans (recipe, left) + 1 cup baby spinach + 2 tbsp coriander leaves + egg.

Meal 3 Cook 2 tsp olive oil + 1 cup corn kernels in a pan for 3 minutes. Line a bowl with 1 jumbo tortilla. Add 1 portion burrito beans (recipe, left) + 1 cup baby spinach + corn.

Meal 4 Heat 2 tsp olive oil in a pan. Cook ½ sliced capsicum + ¼ thinly sliced onion + 1 shredded carrot until soft. Line a bowl with 1 jumbo tortilla. Add 1 portion burrito beans (recipe, left) + 1 cup baby spinach + capsicum mixture + 2 tbsp coriander leaves + 1 tbsp sour cream.

PICK YOUR PROTEIN

CHICKEN

TANDOORI CHICKEN TRAY BAKE

TANDOORI CHICKEN TRAY BAKE

¼ cup (75g) tandoori paste

½ cup (140g) Yo Pro natural yoghurt

8 chicken thigh fillets (1.4kg), trimmed

400g (12½oz) can chickpeas
(garbanzo beans), drained, rinsed

½ large red onion (150g),
cut into wedges

1 small cauliflower (1kg),
cut into wedges, leaves attached

1½ tbsp extra virgin olive oil

100g (3oz) cherry truss tomatoes

60g (2oz) kale leaves

ASSEMBLY INGREDIENTS

¾ cup (210g) Yo Pro natural yoghurt

¼ cup (75g) mango chutney

250g (8oz) baby cucumbers (qukes)

½ large red onion (150g)

150g (4½oz) cherry truss tomatoes

60g (2oz) kale leaves

2 tbsp extra virgin olive oil

lime wedges, to serve

1½ tbsp tandoori paste

125g (4oz) microwave brown rice

2 naan breads (250g)

⭘ MEAL PREP

Tandoori chicken tray bake Preheat oven to 220°C/425°F. Combine tandoori paste + yoghurt + chicken. Place chickpeas + onion in a baking-paper-lined roasting pan. Top with chicken + cauliflower wedges coated with the oil. Bake for 15 minutes. Add tomatoes + kale. Bake for another 10 minutes until vegetables start browning and chicken is cooked.

⭘ STORING

Divide tandoori chicken into 4 portions. Divide roasted chickpeas & onion into 2 portions. Divide cauliflower wedges into 3 portions. Store roasted tomatoes and kale as 1 portion. Refrigerate for up to 4 days.

⭘ ASSEMBLY (SEE PAGE 32)

Meal 1 Tandoori chicken tray bake

Meal 2 Tandoori chicken & kachumber salad

Meal 3 Tandoori chicken pilaf

Meal 4 Tandoori chicken pizza

MEAL 1

TANDOORI CHICKEN TRAY BAKE

Serve 1 portion reheated tandoori chicken, sliced + 1 portion each reheated roasted chickpeas & onion + cauliflower wedges with roasted tomatoes and kale portion. Serve with ¼ cup yoghurt mixed with 1 tbsp mango chutney.

MEAL 2

TANDOORI CHICKEN & KACHUMBER SALAD

Coarsely chop 1 portion cauliflower wedges. Add 1 portion reheated tandoori chicken, sliced. Combine 2 baby cucumbers, quartered + ¼ raw red onion (125g), thinly sliced + 50g (1½oz) fresh cherry tomatoes, sliced + 30g (1oz) fresh kale massaged with 1 tsp oil and a pinch salt; season. Drizzle with more oil and a squeeze of lime. Serve with ¼ cup yoghurt mixed with 1 tbsp mango chutney.

MEAL 3

TANDOORI CHICKEN PILAF

Heat 1 tbsp oil in a frying pan. Cook 1 tbsp tandoori paste + ¼ raw red onion (125g), chopped + rice + 1 portion cauliflower wedges, chopped + 1 portion tandoori chicken, sliced, stirring, for 5 minutes until warmed through. Add 50g (1½oz) fresh cherry tomatoes, quartered + 2 baby cucumbers, chopped.

MEAL 4

TANDOORI CHICKEN PIZZA

Preheat oven to 200°C/400°F. Spread ¼ cup yoghurt + 2 tsp tandoori paste + 1 tbsp mango chutney over naan breads. Add 1 portion roasted chickpeas & onion + 1 portion tandoori chicken, sliced. Bake for 15 minutes until golden and crisp. Top with 30g (1oz) fresh kale tossed in 1 tsp oil + 4 baby cucumbers, sliced lengthways + 50g (1½oz) fresh cherry tomatoes, quartered. Season. Serve with 1 lime wedge.

JAPANESE SESAME CHICKEN & SOBA SALAD

SESAME CHICKEN & BROCCOLINI

8 chicken thigh fillets (1.4kg), trimmed

½ cup (75g) sesame seeds

1 bunch broccolini (175g), trimmed, halved lengthways

SOBA SALAD

180g (5½oz) buckwheat soba noodles, cooked, drained

¼ cup (50g) shelled frozen edamame (soy beans), blanched

150g (4½oz) rainbow coleslaw

2 tbsp white (shiro) miso

2 tbsp mirin

ASSEMBLY INGREDIENTS

3 green onions (scallions), sliced

2 tbsp pickled pink ginger

¾ cup (150g) shelled frozen edamame (soy beans), blanched

3 x 18g (¾oz) sachets instant miso soup with wakame

150g (4½oz) rainbow coleslaw

2 tbsp japanese mayonnaise

1 tbsp white (shiro) miso

¼ cup (60ml) mirin

1 egg, beaten

125g (4oz) microwave brown rice, heated

● MEAL PREP

Sesame chicken & broccolini Coat chicken in sesame seeds. Cook chicken on an oiled grill plate over medium-high heat for 5 minutes each side until cooked through.

Cook broccolini on grill plate for 1 minute each side until just tender.

Soba salad Combine half the cooked noodles (reserve remaining for meal 2) + half the cooked broccolini (reserve remaining for meals 2 and 3) + edamame + coleslaw. Toss with combined miso and mirin.

● STORING

Divide sesame chicken into 4 portions. Divide remaining cooked broccolini into 2 portions. Store soba salad as 1 portion. Refrigerate for up to 4 days.

● ASSEMBLY (SEE PAGE 36)

Meal 1 Japanese sesame chicken & soba salad

Meal 2 Sesame chicken miso noodle soup

Meal 3 Sesame chicken with japanese slaw

Meal 4 Sesame chicken donburi bowl

MEAL 1

JAPANESE SESAME CHICKEN & SOBA SALAD

Serve soba salad portion + 1 portion reheated sesame chicken, sliced + 1 sliced green onion + 1 tbsp pickled ginger.

MEAL 2

SESAME CHICKEN MISO NOODLE SOUP

Stir reserved cooked soba noodles (from soba salad) + ¼ cup edamame + 1 portion broccolini, halved + 2 miso soup sachets + 1 cup boiling water in a bowl. Serve with 1 portion reheated sesame chicken, sliced + 1 sliced green onion.

MEAL 3

SESAME CHICKEN WITH JAPANESE SLAW

Combine 1 portion broccolini, chopped + ¼ cup edamame + 1 tbsp thinly sliced pickled ginger + coleslaw. Combine mayonnaise + white miso + 1 tbsp mirin; stir through slaw. Add 1 portion reheated sesame chicken, sliced.

MEAL 4

SESAME CHICKEN DONBURI BOWL

Bring ½ cup water + 1 miso soup sachet + 2 tbsp mirin to a simmer in a saucepan. Add 1 portion sesame chicken, shredded + ¼ cup edamame. Slowly pour over egg without stirring. Cover; cook over medium heat for 2 minutes until egg is just set. Serve with heated rice + 1 sliced green onion.

SATAY 'POPCORN' CHICKEN

WITH PIMPED SLAW

SATAY 'POPCORN' CHICKEN

**2 chicken breast fillets (400g),
cut into 2cm (¾in) pieces**

¼ cup (75g) satay sauce

**1½ cups (225g) roasted salted peanuts,
chopped finely**

PIMPED SLAW

2 tsp lime juice

½ tsp raw sugar

150g (4½oz) rainbow coleslaw

½ cup thai basil leaves

**1½ cups (225g) roasted salted peanuts,
chopped finely**

ASSEMBLY INGREDIENTS

⅓ cup (75g) japanese mayonnaise

3 tsp sriracha

lime wedges, to serve

**250g (8oz) microwave brown rice,
heated**

2 sheets nori (5g), halved crossways

½ cup thai basil leaves

1½ tbsp vegetable oil

**1 small orange sweet potato (250g),
spiralised (see page 182)**

150g (4¾oz) rainbow coleslaw

**⅓ cup (45g) roasted salted peanuts,
chopped finely**

⬤ MEAL PREP

Satay 'popcorn' chicken Preheat oven to 200°C/400°F. Line a large oven tray with baking paper. Combine chicken + satay sauce; season. Press peanuts onto chicken to coat evenly. Bake on lined tray for 13 minutes until cooked through.

Pimped slaw Meanwhile, combine lime juice + sugar + 1 tsp water; stir to dissolve sugar. Combine lime dressing with coleslaw + thai basil leaves + peanuts.

⬤ STORING

Divide satay 'popcorn' chicken into 4 portions. Divide pimped slaw into 2 portions. Refrigerate for up to 4 days.

⬤ ASSEMBLY (SEE PAGE 40)

Meal 1 Satay 'popcorn' chicken with pimped slaw

Meal 2 'Popcorn' chicken nori cones

Meal 3 'Popcorn' chicken pumpkin noodle pad thai

Meal 4 'Popcorn' chicken fried rice

Tip For Meal 3, instead of making your own sweet potato noodles, use a packet of purchased sweet potato 'spaghetti'.

MEAL 1

SATAY 'POPCORN' CHICKEN WITH PIMPED SLAW

Serve 1 portion reheated satay 'popcorn' chicken + 1 portion pimped slaw + 2 tbsp mayonnaise swirled with 2 tsp sriracha for dipping + 1 lime wedge.

MEAL 2

'POPCORN' CHICKEN NORI CONES

Combine 125g (4oz) heated rice + 1 portion each pimped slaw + reheated satay 'popcorn' chicken + 2 tbsp mayonnaise. Form nori halves into cones; seal ends with a little water. Divide rice mixture among nori cones just before serving. Top with 2 tbsp thai basil leaves.

MEAL 3

'POPCORN' CHICKEN PUMPKIN NOODLE PAD THAI

Heat 2 tsp oil in a frying pan over high heat. Cook sweet potato noodles + 125g (4oz) rainbow coleslaw + 2 tbsp peanuts + 1 portion satay 'popcorn' chicken, stirring, for 4 minutes until sweet potato noodles are tender; season. Top with 2 tbsp thai basil leaves. Serve with 1 lime wedge.

MEAL 4

'POPCORN' CHICKEN FRIED RICE

Heat 1 tbsp oil in a frying pan over high heat. Cook 125g (4oz) heated rice + 1 portion satay 'popcorn' chicken + 25g (¾oz) rainbow coleslaw + 2 tbsp peanuts + 1 tsp sriracha, stirring, for 3 minutes until warmed through. Top with 2 tbsp thai basil leaves. Serve with 1 lime wedge.

ONE-PAN MOROCCAN CHICKEN & VEG

LEMON DRESSING

½ cup (125ml) extra virgin olive oil

2 tbsp moroccan seasoning

1 tbsp finely grated lemon rind

⅓ cup (80ml) lemon juice

MOROCCAN CHICKEN & ROASTED VEG

4 chicken breast fillets (800g), flattened slightly

350g (11oz) vine sweet mini bell peppers, halved

2 medium red onions (340g), cut into thin wedges, 1 wedge reserved

2 medium zucchini (240g), cut into 2cm (¾in) pieces

1 cup (180g) pitted green sicilian olives, drained

CHICKPEA CROUTONS

400g (12½oz) can chickpeas (garbanzo beans), drained, rinsed, patted dry

3 tsp harissa paste

2 tsp extra virgin olive oil

ASSEMBLY INGREDIENTS

250g (8oz) microwave brown rice and quinoa, heated

250g (8oz) persian fetta in oil, crumbled

100g (3oz) mixed salad leaves

1 tbsp harissa paste

1 tsp moroccan seasoning

1 cup (250ml) tomato passata

¼ cup (70g) greek yoghurt

⊙ MEAL PREP

Lemon dressing Combine oil + moroccan seasoning + lemon rind + lemon juice in a screw-top jar.

Moroccan chicken & roasted veg Preheat oven to 220°C/425°F. Place chicken + vegetables + olives + ⅓ cup of the dressing in a baking-paper-lined large roasting pan. Roast for 25 minutes until chicken is cooked; remove chicken. Roast vegetables for a further 10 minutes until browned. Reserve pan juices.

Chickpea croutons Meanwhile, combine half the chickpeas (reserve remaining for meals 3 and 4) + harissa + oil in a baking-paper-lined oven tray; roast for last 15 minutes of chicken and vegetable cooking time or until crisp.

⊙ STORING

Divide moroccan chicken & roasted veg into 4 portions. Divide chickpea croutons into 2 portions. Store remaining lemon dressing in screw-top jar. Refrigerate for up to 4 days.

⊙ ASSEMBLY (SEE PAGE 44)

Meal 1 One-pan moroccan chicken & veg

Meal 2 Moroccan chicken salad & chickpea croutons

Meal 3 Moroccan chicken with chickpea salad

Meal 4 Cheat's chicken tagine

MEAL 1

ONE-PAN MOROCCAN CHICKEN & VEG

Serve 1 portion reheated moroccan chicken & roasted veg + half the reserved pan juices + 125g (4oz) heated rice + 1 portion chickpea croutons + a third of the fetta.

MEAL 2

MOROCCAN CHICKEN SALAD & CHICKPEA CROUTONS

Serve 1 portion reheated moroccan chicken, sliced & roasted veg + 50g (1½oz) salad leaves dressed with 2 tbsp of the lemon dressing + 1 portion chickpea croutons + a third of the fetta.

MEAL 3

MOROCCAN CHICKEN WITH CHICKPEA SALAD

Combine 1 portion reheated moroccan chicken, shredded & roasted veg + half the reserved chickpeas (from chickpea croutons) + 50g (1½oz) salad leaves + reserved red onion wedge, finely chopped + a third of the fetta + 2 tbsp of the lemon dressing mixed with ½ tsp harissa.

MEAL 4

CHEAT'S CHICKEN TAGINE

Cook 1 portion moroccan chicken, thickly sliced & roasted veg + remaining reserved pan juices + morrocan seasoning + remaining reserved chickpeas (from chickpea croutons) + passata + 2 tsp harissa in a saucepan over medium heat for 5 minutes until warmed through. Serve with 125g (4oz) heated rice + yoghurt swirled with 1 tsp harissa.

TEXAN CHICKEN
& SWEET POTATO SKILLET

TEXAN CHICKEN & SWEET POTATO SKILLET

2 tbsp extra virgin olive oil

4 chicken breast fillets (800g), halved horizontally

3 cloves garlic, chopped finely

2 tsp smoked paprika

2 small red capsicums (bell peppers) (300g), quartered

410g (13oz) can tomato puree

2 jalapeño chillies (40g), sliced

3 small purple sweet potatoes (600g), sliced into thin rounds

ASSEMBLY INGREDIENTS

120g (4oz) mixed salad leaves

2 tbsp extra virgin olive oil

2 tsp lime juice

1 cup (250ml) chicken stock

250g (8oz) cauliflower rice (see tip)

1 egg

½ cup (60g) frozen peas

lime wedges, to serve

½ cup (120g) spreadable cream cheese, heated gently in microwave for 30 seconds

○ MEAL PREP

Texan chicken & sweet potato skillet Heat oil in large heavy-based frying pan over high heat. Cook chicken, turning, for 3 minutes until golden. Add garlic + paprika + capsicum; cook for 2 minutes. Stir in tomato puree + ½ cup water + jalapeño. Place sweet potato on top in a single layer. Cover tightly with foil. Cook over low heat for 20 minutes until chicken is cooked through.

○ STORING

Divide texan chicken and sweet potato, separately, into 4 portions. Refrigerate for up to 4 days.

○ ASSEMBLY (SEE PAGE 48)

Meal 1 Texan chicken & sweet potato skillet

Meal 2 Texan skillet chicken pozole

Meal 3 Texan chicken fried 'rice'

Meal 4 Texan chicken 'nachos'

Tip To make your own cauliflower rice, see page 171, or use purchased frozen cauliflower rice instead.

MEAL 1

TEXAN CHICKEN & SWEET POTATO SKILLET

Serve 1 portion reheated texan chicken + 60g (2oz) salad leaves dressed with 3 tsp oil + 1 tsp lime juice. Top with 1 portion sweet potato.

MEAL 2

TEXAN SKILLET CHICKEN POZOLE

Shred 1 portion texan chicken and thinly slice the cooked capsicum. Heat texan chicken mixture + sliced cooked capsicum + stock + 125g (4oz) cauliflower rice in a small saucepan. Top with 1 portion sweet potato. Season.

MEAL 3

TEXAN CHICKEN FRIED 'RICE'

Chop 1 portion texan chicken and the cooked capsicum. Heat 1 tsp oil in a non-stick frying pan over medium heat. Fry egg for 2 minutes until partially set; break up in pan. Add the texan chicken mixture + chopped cooked capsicum + 125g (4oz) cauliflower rice + peas; stir for 3 minutes until hot. Top with 1 portion sweet potato. Serve with 1 lime wedge. Season.

MEAL 4

TEXAN CHICKEN 'NACHOS'

Preheat oven to 200°C/400°F. Shred 1 portion texan chicken and slice the cooked capsicum. Place the texan chicken mixture + sliced cooked capsicum in a 2-cup ovenproof dish. Spread heated cream cheese over mixture; arrange 1 portion sweet potato on top. Bake for 15 minutes until golden and bubbling. Serve with 60g (2oz) salad leaves dressed with 3 tsp oil + 1 tsp lime juice. Season to taste.

FEELING SAUCY

Combine all ingredients, then season with sea salt and black pepper to taste.

ROCKIN' GUACAMOLE

PREP TIME 10 MINUTES MAKES 2 CUPS

Mash 2 medium avocados (500g) in a bowl. Stir in 1 finely chopped small fresh long red chilli + 1 crushed small garlic clove + 1 tbsp lime juice + ½ cup finely chopped coriander (cilantro) + ¼ tsp spirulina (optional).

CLASSIC PESTO

PREP TIME 10 MINUTES MAKES 1½ CUPS

Blend or process 2 cups firmly packed basil leaves + ½ cup (40g) finely grated parmesan + ¼ cup (35g) toasted pine nuts + 1 small clove crushed garlic + ¾ cup extra virgin olive oil until smooth.

ROMESCO

PREP TIME 10 MINUTES MAKES 2 CUPS

Process 260g (8½oz) drained jar of roasted red capsicums (bell peppers) + 1 clove crushed garlic + ½ cup (70g) roasted blanched almonds + 2 tbsp sherry vinegar + 1 tsp smoked paprika + 2 tbsp chopped flat-leaf parsley + ⅓ cup extra virgin olive oil until smooth; season to taste.

JAPANESE DRESSING

PREP TIME 10 MINUTES MAKES 1 CUP

Combine 5cm (2in) piece fresh ginger, finely grated + ¼ cup extra virgin olive oil + 2 tbsp lime juice + ¼ cup mirin + ¼ cup soy sauce + 1 tbsp finely grated palm sugar + 1 finely chopped fresh small red chilli in a screw-top jar.

GREEN HUMMUS
PREP TIME 10 MINUTES MAKES 2 CUPS

Process 1 cup thawed frozen peas + 400g (12½oz) can drained, rinsed chickpeas (garbanzo beans) + 2 tbsp reserved chickpea liquid + 1 clove chopped garlic + 1 cup flat-leaf parsley leaves + ¼ cup lemon juice + 2 tbsp hulled tahini + ¼ cup extra virgin olive oil until smooth; season.

AMAZING GREEN SAUCE
PREP TIME 10 MINUTES MAKES 2 CUPS

Blend or process 1 small chopped avocado (200g) + ¾ cup firmly packed coriander (cilantro) leaves + ½ cup firmly packed flat-leaf parsley leaves + ¼ cup (35g) unsalted pistachios + 1 chopped fresh long green chilli + 1 clove crushed garlic + 2 tbsp lemon juice.

SALSA VERDE
PREP TIME 15 MINUTES MAKES 1½ CUPS

Process 2 cups firmly packed flat-leaf parsley leaves + 1½ tbsp loosely packed lemon thyme leaves + 1 tbsp drained capers + 1 clove crushed garlic + 1 tsp caster (superfine) sugar + ½ cup extra virgin olive oil + 1½ tbsp white wine vinegar until combined.

SIMPLE VINAIGRETTE
PREP TIME 10 MINUTES MAKES ½ CUP

Whisk together ⅓ cup extra virgin olive oil + 2 tbsp white wine vinegar + 1 tbsp dijon mustard + 2 tsp finely grated lemon rind. Season to taste.

CHIPOTLE CHICKEN
& SOUR CREAM POTATOES

CHIPOTLE CHICKEN & SOUR CREAM POTATOES

4 chicken breast fillets (800g)

455g (14½oz) jar black bean and chipotle salsa

1 tbsp extra virgin olive oil

500g (1lb) baby (chat) potatoes, quartered

½ cup (120g) sour cream

CHIPOTLE BEANS

1 tbsp extra virgin olive oil

1 large red onion (300g), cut into thin wedges

2 x 400g (12½oz) cans four-bean mix, drained, rinsed

ASSEMBLY INGREDIENTS

½ small butter (boston) lettuce

lime wedges, to serve

2 pieces mountain bread (50g)

⅓ cup coriander (cilantro) leaves

1 cup (120g) grated cheddar

2 tbsp sour cream

1 tsp extra virgin olive oil

1 small avocado (200g)

1 tbsp lime juice

1 trimmed corn cob (250g), cooked, cut into 4 pieces

O MEAL PREP

Chipotle chicken & sour cream potatoes Preheat oven to 210°C/410°F. Place chicken on a baking-paper-lined oven tray; brush with ½ cup chipotle salsa (reserve remaining for chipotle beans) + oil. Combine potatoes + sour cream and season; place around chicken. Bake for 25 minutes until chicken and potatoes are cooked through.

Chipotle beans Meanwhile, heat oil in a saucepan over high heat. Cook onion for 4 minutes. Add reserved chipotle salsa (from chipotle chicken) + beans + ½ cup water. Reduce heat to low; cover and cook for 15 minutes. Season. Remove lid and cook for a further 8 minutes until thickened.

O STORING

Divide chipotle chicken, sour cream potatoes and chipotle beans, separately, into 4 portions. Refrigerate for up to 4 days.

O ASSEMBLY (SEE PAGE 54)

Meal 1 Chipotle chicken & sour cream potatoes

Meal 2 Chipotle chicken & bean quesadilla

Meal 3 Shredded chipotle chicken with cheesy croutons

Meal 4 Chipotle chicken mexican salad

MEAL 1

CHIPOTLE CHICKEN & SOUR CREAM POTATOES

Serve 1 portion each reheated chipotle chicken, sour cream potatoes and chipotle beans + 1 lettuce leaf + 1 lime wedge.

MEAL 2

CHIPOTLE CHICKEN & BEAN QUESADILLA

Preheat oven to 180°C/350°F. Place 1 mountain bread on a baking-paper-lined tray. Top with 1 portion each sliced chipotle chicken, chipotle beans and sour cream potatoes + 2 tbsp coriander leaves + ½ cup cheddar, placed across a short edge. Fold over to enclose filling, fold in sides, then roll up to create a parcel. Bake for 10 minutes until golden and warmed through. Serve with 1 tbsp sour cream + 1 lime wedge.

MEAL 3

SHREDDED CHIPOTLE CHICKEN WITH CHEESY CROUTONS

Preheat oven to 180°C/350°F. Brush 1 mountain bread with oil; halve widthways, then cut into 2cm (¾in) wide strips. Scatter with ½ cup cheddar. Bake for 4 minutes until crisp. Serve croutons with 1 portion reheated chipotle chicken, shredded, combined with 1 portion each chipotle beans and sour cream potatoes + ½ avocado mashed with lime juice. Top with 1 tbsp coriander leaves.

MEAL 4

CHIPOTLE CHICKEN MEXICAN SALAD

Slice 1 portion reheated chipotle chicken. Serve with 1 portion each reheated sour cream potatoes and chipotle beans + 1 lettuce leaf + corn + ½ avocado, sliced. Serve with 1 tbsp sour cream mixed with 1 tbsp chopped coriander + 1 lime wedge.

GRILLED MUSTARD-LEMON CHICKEN & SWEET POTATO

DRESSING

2 lemons

½ cup (125ml) extra virgin olive oil

2 tbsp wholegrain mustard

GRILLED MUSTARD-LEMON CHICKEN & SWEET POTATO

1 tbsp fennel seeds, crushed

4 chicken breast fillets (800g)

3 small orange sweet potatoes (750g)

FENNEL SLAW

1 baby fennel bulb (130g), fronds reserved

150g (4½oz) brussels sprouts

ASSEMBLY INGREDIENTS

250g (8oz) mixed cherry tomatoes, halved

2 tbsp extra virgin olive oil

1 baby fennel bulb (130g), shaved, fronds reserved

150g (4½oz) brussels sprouts, shaved

¼ tsp fennel seeds, crushed

250g (8oz) packet frozen cauliflower rice

60g (2oz) baby rocket (arugula)

⅓ cup (90g) pesto

lemon wedges, to serve

1 small orange sweet potato (250g)

◯ MEAL PREP

Dressing Finely grate 1 tbsp lemon rind and squeeze ¼ cup juice from lemons; combine with oil + mustard in a screw-top jar. Season.

Grilled mustard-lemon chicken & sweet potato Rub fennel seeds over chicken. Cook chicken on a hot oiled grill plate over medium-high heat for 8 minutes each side until cooked; set aside.

Cut sweet potatoes thinly lengthways with a V-slicer or mandoline; coat in ¼ cup of the dressing. Cook sweet potato on hot oiled grill for 2 minutes each side until tender and grill lines appear.

Fennel slaw Meanwhile, shave fennel bulb + brussels sprouts with a V-slicer or mandoline. Toss in 2 tbsp of the dressing; season.

◯ STORING

Divide mustard-lemon chicken into 4 portions. Divide sweet potato into 3 portions. Store fennel slaw as 1 portion. Store remaining dressing in screw-top jar. Refrigerate for up to 4 days.

◯ ASSEMBLY (SEE PAGE 58)

Meal 1 Grilled mustard-lemon chicken & sweet potato

Meal 2 Grilled chicken & warm cauli rice salad

Meal 3 Grilled chicken nourishing bowl

Meal 4 Grilled chicken & sweet potato pesto voodles

Tip For meal 4, instead of making your own sweet potato noodles, use a packet of purchased sweet potato 'spaghetti'.

MEAL 1

GRILLED MUSTARD-LEMON CHICKEN & SWEET POTATO

Serve 1 portion each reheated mustard-lemon chicken, thickly sliced, and sweet potato with fennel slaw portion; season. Serve with a quarter of the cherry tomatoes. Drizzle with 2 tbsp of the dressing.

MEAL 2

GRILLED CHICKEN & WARM CAULI RICE SALAD

Heat 1 tbsp oil in a frying pan. Cook shaved fennel + shaved brussels sprouts for 3 minutes until golden; set aside. Add 1 tbsp oil to pan + fennel seeds + 125g (4oz) cauliflower rice; cook for 2 minutes until hot. Serve with 1 portion reheated mustard-lemon chicken, sliced + 1 portion sweet potato + a quarter of the cherry tomatoes + 20g (¾oz) rocket. Drizzle with 2 tbsp of the dressing.

MEAL 3

GRILLED CHICKEN NOURISHING BOWL

Heat 125g (4oz) cauliflower rice; add 1 tbsp pesto. Serve with 1 portion reheated mustard-lemon chicken, thickly sliced lengthways + 1 portion sweet potato, cut into strips + a quarter of the cherry tomatoes + 20g (¾oz) rocket; season. Drizzle with 2 tbsp of the dressing. Serve with 1 lemon wedge.

MEAL 4

GRILLED CHICKEN & SWEET POTATO PESTO VOODLES

Spiralise whole sweet potato (see page 182); boil, steam or microwave voodles until tender; drain. Mix voodles with ¼ cup pesto mixed with 1 tbsp hot water to loosen; season. Serve with 1 portion reheated mustard-lemon chicken, sliced + a quarter of the cherry tomatoes + 20g (¾oz) rocket + reserved fennel fronds + 1 lemon wedge.

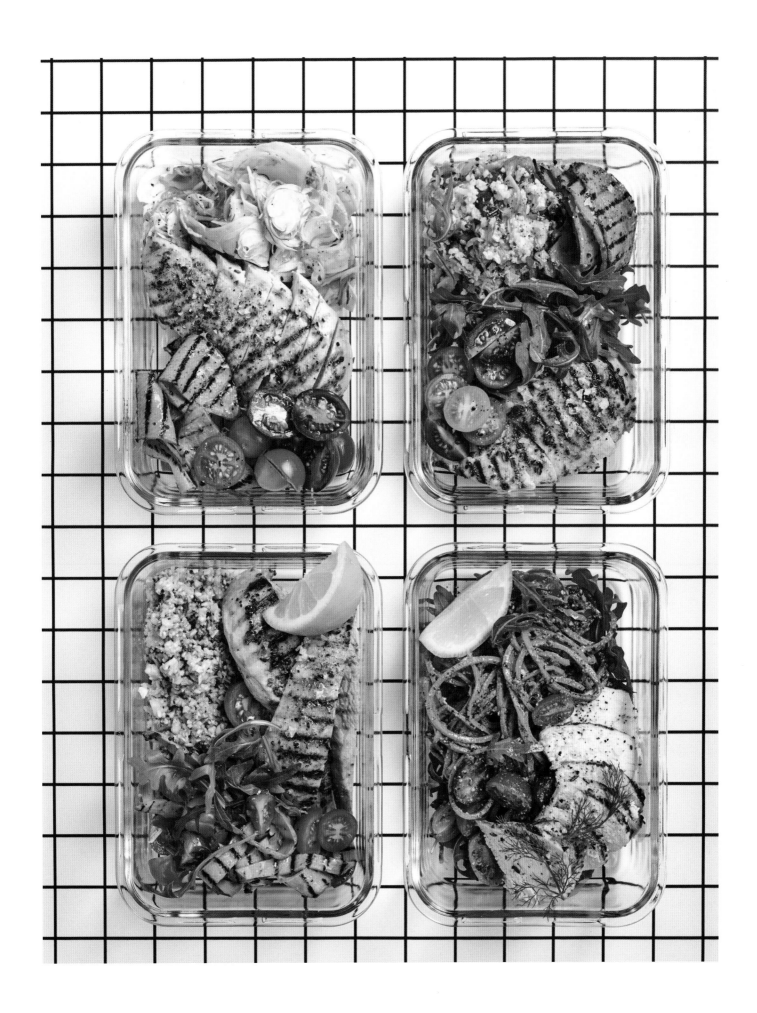

TURMERIC-HONEY CHICKEN

WITH COCONUT SWEET POTATO

COCONUT SWEET POTATO

4 small orange sweet potatoes (1kg), halved lengthways

400ml can coconut milk

TURMERIC-HONEY CHICKEN & BROCCOLINI

3 chicken breast fillets (600g), cut into quarters lengthways

1 tbsp honey

2 tsp ground turmeric

2 tbsp olive oil

2 bunches broccolini (350g), trimmed

ASSEMBLY INGREDIENTS

2 tbsp chopped roasted salted cashews

450g (14½oz) korma simmer sauce

½ cup (140g) greek yoghurt

75g (2½oz) packet ready-to-eat mini pappadums

1 tbsp chopped coriander (cilantro), plus 2 tbsp leaves

● MEAL PREP

Coconut sweet potato Preheat oven to 220°C/425°F. Place a large piece of foil on an oven tray; top with sweet potato and season. Fold foil over sweet potato, then fold in edges to seal and create a pouch. Pour coconut milk into top opening; seal completely. Bake for 30 minutes until tender. Reserve liquid.

Turmeric-honey chicken & broccolini Meanwhile, combine chicken + honey + turmeric + oil on a baking-paper-lined ovenproof tray; season. Thread a chicken piece lengthways onto each of 12 skewers. Cook on a hot oiled grill plate over medium-high heat for 3 minutes each side until cooked through. Set aside.

Chargrill broccolini on heated grill plate for 1 minute until tender but stil crisp.

● STORING

Divide coconut sweet potato and the reserved cooking liquid, turmeric-honey chicken and broccolini, separately, into 4 portions. Refrigerate for up to 4 days.

● ASSEMBLY (SEE PAGE 62)

Meal 1 Turmeric-honey chicken with coconut sweet potato

Meal 2 Turmeric chicken korma

Meal 3 Loaded turmeric chicken sweet potato

Meal 4 Sweet potato korma soup with turmeric chicken

MEAL 1

TURMERIC-HONEY CHICKEN WITH COCONUT SWEET POTATO

Serve 1 portion each reheated coconut sweet potato + turmeric-honey chicken + broccolini, halved + 2 tbsp of the reserved cooking liquid. Top with 1 tbsp cashews. Season.

MEAL 2

TURMERIC CHICKEN KORMA

Bring ½ jar korma simmer sauce + ⅓ cup water to a simmer in a small saucepan. Chop 1 portion each broccolini, turmeric-honey chicken and coconut sweet potato; add to pan. Cook for 2 minutes until warmed through; season. Top with 2 tbsp yoghurt + 1 tbsp chopped cashews. Serve with half a packet of pappadams.

MEAL 3

LOADED TURMERIC CHICKEN SWEET POTATO

Combine 1 portion turmeric-honey chicken, shredded + 1 portion broccolini, chopped + 1 tbsp of the reserved cooking liquid; season. Reheat chicken mixture with 1 portion coconut sweet potato. Top with 2 tbsp yoghurt mixed with chopped coriander; season.

MEAL 4

SWEET POTATO KORMA SOUP WITH TURMERIC CHICKEN

Chop 1 portion coconut sweet potato. Combine with remaining ½ jar korma simmer sauce + remaining reserved cooking liquid + 1½ cups water in a saucepan. Bring to the boil; cook for 2 minutes until warmed through. Blend until smooth. Top with 1 portion each turmeric-honey chicken and broccolini, chopped. Top with 2 tbsp each yoghurt + coriander leaves. Serve with half a packet of pappadams.

SPICED CHICKEN PATTIES

WITH BEETROOT & RICE SALAD

SPICED CHICKEN PATTIES

1kg (2lb) minced (ground) chicken

250g (8oz) microwave brown rice and quinoa, heated

2 eggs, beaten lightly

1 tbsp finely grated lemon rind

2 tsp ground cumin

½ cup chopped coriander (cilantro)

BEETROOT & RICE SALAD

125g (4oz) microwave brown rice and quinoa, heated

4 pickled baby beetroot (beets) (250g)

½ baby cos (romaine) lettuce (65g)

70g (2½oz) fetta, crumbled

⅓ cup (80ml) extra virgin olive oil

2 tbsp lemon juice

1 tbsp finely grated lemon rind

ASSEMBLY INGREDIENTS

½ cup (140g) tzatziki

½ cup (125ml) coconut milk

1 tbsp green curry paste

½ cup (125ml) chicken stock

50g (1½oz) snow peas, halved

125g (4oz) microwave brown rice and quinoa, heated

2 tbsp coriander (cilantro) leaves

2 wholemeal roti (120g)

½ baby cos (romaine) lettuce (65g)

2 medium tomatoes (300g)

4 baby cucumbers (qukes) (120g)

130g (4oz) fetta, crumbled

O MEAL PREP

Spiced chicken patties Mix mince + slightly cooled rice + egg + lemon rind + cumin + coriander in a bowl. Shape mixture into 12 patties. Cook patties in an oiled large non-stick frying pan over medium heat for 4 minutes each side until cooked through.

Beetroot & rice salad Place heated rice + beetroot cut into wedges + lettuce leaves + fetta in a bowl. Combine oil + lemon juice + lemon rind in a screw-top jar. Add 2 tbsp dressing to rice mixture and season (reserve remaining dressing for meals 3 and 4).

O STORING

Divide spiced chicken patties into 4 portions. Store beetroot & rice salad as 1 portion. Store remaining dressing in screw-top jar. Refrigerate for up to 4 days.

O ASSEMBLY (SEE PAGE 66)

Meal 1 Spiced chicken patties with beetroot & rice salad

Meal 2 Green chicken pattie curry

Meal 3 Chicken pattie roti

Meal 4 Chicken patties with greek salad

MEAL 1

SPICED CHICKEN PATTIES WITH BEETROOT & RICE SALAD

Serve 1 portion reheated spiced chicken patties with beetroot & rice salad portion + 2 tbsp tzatziki.

MEAL 2

GREEN CHICKEN PATTIE CURRY

Cook coconut milk + curry paste in a wok over high heat for 1 minute. Add stock + 1 portion spiced chicken patties, quartered + snow peas + heated rice; cook for 2 minutes until warmed through. Top with coriander leaves.

MEAL 3

CHICKEN PATTIE ROTI

Spread warmed roti each with 2 tbsp tzatziki; top with 1 portion reheated spiced chicken patties, sliced. Add 2 lettuce leaves, shredded + 1 tomato, chopped + 2 baby cucumbers, chopped; drizzle with 2 tbsp of the reserved dressing (from beetroot & rice salad). Top with 65g (2oz) fetta.

MEAL 4

CHICKEN PATTIES WITH GREEK SALAD

Cut remaining lettuce into wedges. Serve with 2 baby cucumbers, thickly sliced + 1 tomato, cut into wedges + 65g (2oz) fetta + 1 portion spiced chicken patties, cut into chunks. Drizzle with 2 tbsp of the reserved dressing (from beetroot & rice salad); season.

PICK YOUR PROTEIN

SALMON

CHILLI-GLAZED SALMON
WITH KIMCHI CORN

CHILLI-GLAZED SALMON

olive oil cooking spray

2 tbsp pure maple syrup

2 tbsp gochujang (korean fermented chilli paste)

4 x 200g (6½oz) boneless salmon fillets, skin on

KIMCHI CORN

50g (1½oz) butter, softened

1½ tbsp kimchi, drained (1 tbsp liquid reserved), chopped finely

3 trimmed corn cobs (750g)

ASSEMBLY INGREDIENTS

3 small zucchini (270g)

¼ cup (25g) kimchi, drained

8 radishes (280g), shaved

3 regular wholegrain tortillas

½ cup (140g) greek yoghurt

400g (12½oz) can red kidney beans, drained (¼ cup liquid reserved), rinsed

¼ cup coriander (cilantro) leaves

1 tsp gochujang (korean fermented chilli paste)

1 egg, hard-boiled (see page 183)

lime wedges, to serve

○ **MEAL PREP**

Chilli-glazed salmon Preheat oven grill to high. Line two oven trays with foil; spray with oil. Combine maple syrup + gochujang; season. Reserve a third of the mixture. Rub salmon with remaining gochujang mixture. Place on one lined tray. Grill salmon, without turning, for 5 minutes until just cooked through. Brush with the reserved gochujang mixture.

Kimchi corn Combine butter and chopped kimchi. Rub corn with half the kimchi butter (reserve remaining butter for meal 2); place on second lined tray. Grill corn, turning halfway through cooking time, for 5 minutes until browned evenly.

○ **STORING**

Divide chilli-glazed salmon into 4 portions. Divide kimchi corn into 3 portions. Refrigerate for up to 4 days.

○ **ASSEMBLY (SEE PAGE 72)**

Meal 1 Chilli-glazed salmon with kimchi corn

Meal 2 Korean salmon zoodle bowl

Meal 3 Kimchi salmon tacos

Meal 4 Korean beans & egg bowl

MEAL 1

CHILLI-GLAZED SALMON WITH KIMCHI CORN

Cut 2 zucchini lengthways into ribbons. Combine with 1 tbsp reserved kimchi liquid; season. Serve 1 portion reheated chilli-glazed salmon + 1 portion kimchi corn + 1 tbsp kimchi.

MEAL 2

KOREAN SALMON ZOODLE BOWL

Spiralise 1 zucchini (see page 182). Heat remaining kimchi butter (from kimchi corn) in a non-stick frying pan for 2 minutes until starting to soften. Add kernels cut from 1 portion kimchi corn; cook until warmed through. Serve 1 portion reheated chilli-glazed salmon with zoodles + kimchi corn kernels + 4 shaved radishes.

MEAL 3

KIMCHI SALMON TACOS

Cut kernels from 1 portion kimchi corn. Spread 2 warmed tortillas each with 2 tbsp yoghurt. Divide kimchi corn kernels + 1 portion reheated chilli-glazed salmon, flaked + half the kidney beans + 2 shaved radishes + 2 tbsp kimchi + 2 tbsp coriander leaves between tortillas.

MEAL 4

KOREAN BEANS & EGG BOWL

Heat remaining kidney beans + the ¼ cup reserved canning liquid + gochujang in a saucepan. Serve with 1 portion reheated chilli-glazed salmon + hard-boiled egg, quartered + 2 shaved radishes + 1 warmed tortilla. Top with 1 tbsp greek yoghurt + 1 tbsp coriander leaves. Serve with 1 lime wedge.

CHIPOTLE SALMON
WITH LIME CORN & PICO DE GALLO

LIME CORN

4 corn cobs (1kg),
husks and silks removed

2 tbsp extra virgin olive oil

2 tsp finely grated lime rind

PICO DE GALLO

2 medium tomatoes (300g),
chopped finely

1 small red onion (100g), chopped finely

⅓ cup finely chopped coriander
(cilantro)

1 tbsp lime juice

CHIPOTLE SALMON

4 x 200g (6½oz) skinless boneless
salmon fillets

1 tsp chipotle tabasco sauce

2 tbsp extra virgin olive oil

ASSEMBLY INGREDIENTS

⅓ cup coriander (cilantro) leaves

lime wedges or cheeks, to serve

175g (5½oz) vine sweet mini capsicums
(bell peppers), halved

1 tsp chipotle tabasco sauce

2 regular wholegrain tortillas, warmed

1 tbsp extra virgin olive oil

3 eggs, beaten lightly

125g (4oz) microwave brown
and wild rice, heated

⭘ MEAL PREP

Lime corn Grill corn on a hot grill plate, turning, over high heat for
20 minutes until charred evenly. Combine oil + lime rind; season.
Brush corn with lime oil.

Pico de gallo Meanwhile, combine tomato + onion + coriander
+ lime juice; season.

Chipotle salmon Combine salmon + tabasco sauce + oil; season.
Grill salmon on a baking-paper-lined grill plate over high heat for
2½ minutes each side until just cooked through.

⭘ STORING

Divide lime corn, pico de gallo and chipotle salmon, separately,
into 4 portions. Refrigerate for up to 4 days.

⭘ ASSEMBLY (SEE PAGE 76)

Meal 1 Chipotle salmon with lime corn & pico de gallo

Meal 2 Chipotle salmon tortillas

Meal 3 Salmon frittata mexicana

Meal 4 Chipotle salmon 'burrito' bowl

MEAL 1

CHIPOTLE SALMON WITH LIME CORN & PICO DE GALLO

Serve 1 portion reheated chipotle salmon
+ 1 portion lime corn, cut into thirds
+ 1 portion pico de gallo. Top with 2 tbsp
coriander leaves + 1 lime wedge.

MEAL 2

CHIPOTLE SALMON TORTILLAS

Cook capsicum in an oiled frying pan over
medium-high heat for 4 minutes until softened
(reserve half the cooked capsicum and
refrigerate for meal 3). Add tabasco sauce to
remaining capsicum in the pan. Add 1 portion
chipotle salmon, flaked, to warm through. Divide
salmon mixture + 1 portion lime corn kernels
+ 1 portion pico de gallo between chargrilled
tortillas. Serve with 1 lime cheek.

MEAL 3

SALMON FRITTATA MEXICANA

Heat oil in a small frying pan (base measurement
15cm/6in) over high heat. Add egg + 1 portion
chipotle salmon, flaked + reserved cooked
capsicum (from meal 2). Reduce heat to
low-medium; cover and cook for 3 minutes
until just cooked through. Top with 1 portion
pico de gallo + 1 portion lime corn kernels.

MEAL 4

CHIPOTLE SALMON 'BURRITO' BOWL

Serve heated rice + 1 portion reheated chipotle
salmon, flaked + 1 portion lime corn kernels
+ 1 portion pico de gallo. Top with 2 tbsp
coriander leaves.

MIDDLE EASTERN SALMON

WITH GRILLED EGGPLANT SALAD

MIDDLE EASTERN SALMON

¼ cup (75g) pomegranate molasses

⅓ cup (80ml) extra virgin olive oil

4 x 200g (6½oz) skinless boneless salmon fillets

GRILLED EGGPLANT SALAD

2 medium eggplants (600g), cut into 1cm (¾in) rounds

2 large zucchini (300g), sliced lengthways

1 medium red capsicum (bell pepper) (200g), cut into eighths

2 tbsp extra virgin olive oil

1 small navel orange (190g), rind finely grated, then juiced

2 tsp ground cumin

1 tsp ground sumac

ASSEMBLY INGREDIENTS

½ cup (100g) couscous, cooked

400g (12½oz) can chickpeas (garbanzo beans), drained, rinsed, patted dry

½ lemon, juiced

1 cup (25g) trimmed watercress sprigs

½ cup (140g) greek yoghurt

2 white pitta pockets (200g)

1 small lebanese cucumber (100g)

1 tbsp pomegranate seeds

¼ cup chopped mint, plus leaves to serve

◯ MEAL PREP

Middle eastern salmon Combine molasses + oil; brush salmon with 2 tbsp of mixture (reserve remainder for pomegranate dressing). Cook salmon on a baking-paper-lined heated grill pan for 3 minutes each side until just cooked through.

Grilled eggplant salad Combine vegetables + oil + 2 tsp orange rind (reserve juice for pomegranate dressing) + spices; season. Cook in heated grill pan, in batches, for 4 minutes each side for eggplant and capsicum, and 3 minutes each side for zucchini, until charred and tender.

Pomegranate dressing Whisk reserved pomegranate mixture (from middle eastern salmon) + 2 tbsp orange juice (from grilled eggplant salad) in a small bowl.

◯ STORING

Divide middle eastern salmon and grilled eggplant salad, separately, into 4 portions. Store pomegranate dressing in a screw-top jar. Refrigerate for up to 4 days.

◯ ASSEMBLY (SEE PAGE 80)

Meal 1 Middle eastern salmon with grilled eggplant salad

Meal 2 Salmon fattoush salad

Meal 3 Middle eastern salmon pitta pocket

Meal 4 Middle eastern salmon couscous salad

MEAL 1

MIDDLE EASTERN SALMON WITH GRILLED EGGPLANT SALAD

Combine ¼ cup (50g) couscous + half the chickpeas + lemon juice + ½ cup watercress. Serve with 1 portion reheated middle eastern salmon + 1 portion grilled eggplant salad. Top with 2 tbsp yoghurt. Drizzle over 2 tbsp pomegranate dressing. Season.

MEAL 2

SALMON FATTOUSH SALAD

Preheat oven to 180°C/350°F. Mix remaining chickpeas with 2 tsp pomegranate dressing; place on one side of a baking-paper-lined tray. Add 1 coarsely torn pitta to other side. Bake for 10 minutes until golden and crisp. Mix roasted chickpeas + crisp pitta + 1 portion reheated middle eastern salmon, flaked + 1 portion grilled eggplant salad + ½ cucumber, sliced + pomegranate seeds. Drizzle over 1½ tbsp pomegranate dressing. Top with mint leaves.

MEAL 3

MIDDLE EASTERN SALMON PITTA POCKET

Divide 1 portion reheated middle eastern salmon, flaked + 1 portion grilled eggplant salad + 2 tbsp yoghurt between 1 halved pitta pocket. Serve with remaining ½ cucumber, cut into batons. Season.

MEAL 4

MIDDLE EASTERN SALMON COUSCOUS SALAD

Combine ¼ cup (50g) couscous + ½ cup watercress + 1 portion grilled eggplant salad + chopped mint + 2 tbsp pomegranate dressing. Serve with 1 portion reheated middle eastern salmon. Top with 2 tbsp yoghurt + mint leaves. Season to taste.

PREP & COOK TIME | MAKES
20 MINUTES | 4 PORTIONS

TERIYAKI SALMON
WITH SESAME & GINGER GREENS

TERIYAKI SALMON

⅓ cup (80ml) teriyaki sauce

1 tbsp sesame oil

4 x 150g (4½oz) boneless
salmon fillets, skin on

SESAME & GINGER GREENS

1 bunch gai lan (500g), trimmed

1 bunch broccolini (175g), trimmed

2 bunches asparagus (340g), trimmed

2 tsp sesame oil

2 tbsp sesame seeds, toasted

ASSEMBLY INGREDIENTS

2 large eggs, 1 soft-boiled
(see page 183)

1 cup (200g) frozen shelled edamame
(soy beans), blanched

3 tsp sesame seeds, toasted

250g (8oz) microwave brown rice
and quinoa, heated

4 red radishes (70g), shaved

2 baby cucumbers (qukes) (60g)

1 cup (250ml) chicken stock

100g (3oz) fresh shiitake mushrooms,
sliced

90g (3oz) ramen noodles, cooked

⭘ MEAL PREP

Teriyaki salmon Preheat oven to 200°C/400°F. Mix teriyaki sauce + sesame oil (reserve 2 tbsp teriyaki dressing for the meals). Pat salmon dry with paper towel, then brush evenly with remaining teriyaki dressing; season. Roast, skin-side up, on a baking-paper-lined tray for 13 minutes until sticky and just cooked. Brush salmon, with any dressing left on base of tray.

Sesame & ginger greens Meanwhile, cut vegetables into 8cm (1½in) lengths. Toss with sesame oil + sesame seeds. Place on a baking-paper-lined roasting pan; cover with foil. Roast for 10 minutes until tender but still crisp.

⭘ STORING

Divide teriyaki salmon and sesame & ginger greens, separately, into 4 portions. Refrigerate for up to 4 days.

⭘ ASSEMBLY (SEE PAGE 84)

Meal 1 Teriyaki salmon with sesame & ginger greens

Meal 2 Teriyaki salmon power bowl

Meal 3 Teriyaki salmon congee

Meal 4 Teriyaki salmon noodle salad

MEAL 1

TERIYAKI SALMON WITH SESAME & GINGER GREENS

Fry the uncooked egg until the white is firm. Combine 1 portion sesame & ginger greens + ⅓ cup edamame + 1 tsp teriyaki dressing. Add 1 portion reheated teriyaki salmon. Top with fried egg + 1 tsp sesame seeds.

MEAL 2

TERIYAKI SALMON POWER BOWL

Combine 125g (4oz) heated rice + ⅓ cup edamame. Add 1 portion sesame & ginger greens + 1 portion reheated teriyaki salmon. Top with 2 shaved radishes + 1 baby cucumber, diced. Drizzle with 1 tsp teriyaki dressing.

MEAL 3

TERIYAKI SALMON CONGEE

Bring 125g (4oz) rice + stock + mushrooms to the boil in a saucepan. Cover and simmer for 8 minutes until thickened and rice is very soft. Add 1 portion reheated teriyaki salmon, flaked + 1 portion sesame & ginger greens + the soft-boiled egg, sliced, drizzled with 1 tsp teriyaki dressing. Top with 1 tsp sesame seeds.

MEAL 4

TERIYAKI SALMON NOODLE SALAD

Combine noodles with 1 tbsp teriyaki dressing + ⅓ cup edamame + 1 baby cucumber, chopped. Add 1 portion sesame & ginger greens + 1 portion reheated teriyaki salmon, flaked. Top with 2 shaved radishes + 1 tsp sesame seeds.

CLEVER CONDIMENTS

RAITA

PREP TIME 5 MINUTES (+ REFRIGERATION)
MAKES 1¾ CUPS

Place a fine sieve over a bowl; spoon in 500g (1lb) greek yoghurt + ½ tsp salt. Cover and refrigerate for 2 hours until thicker; discard liquid. Meanwhile, combine 1 peeled coarsely grated lebanese cucumber + 1½ tsp salt; stand for 20 minutes, then squeeze out excess liquid. Combine thickened yoghurt + grated cucumber + 1 clove crushed garlic + 2 tbsp chopped mint; season.

MANGO CHUTNEY YOGHURT

PREP TIME 5 MINUTES **MAKES** 1¼ CUPS

Combine 1 cup (280g) greek yoghurt + 2 tsp lemon juice; season. Swirl through 2 tbsp purchased mango chutney. Season to taste.

BASIL & ROCKET YOGHURT

PREP TIME 5 MINUTES **MAKES** 1 CUP

Place 2 cups firmly packed basil leaves + 1 cup baby rocket (arugula) in a heatproof bowl; cover with boiling water. Stand for 1 minute; drain and refresh in ice-cold water. Drain; squeeze out excess water. Blend with ¾ cup (210g) greek yoghurt + 1 tbsp lemon juice until smooth. Season.

TAHINI YOGHURT

PREP TIME 5 MINUTES **MAKES** 1 CUP

Combine 1 small crushed clove garlic + 2 tbsp lemon juice + 2 tbsp tahini + ¾ cup (210g) greek yoghurt + 1 tbsp shredded mint; season.

KOREAN MAYO

PREP TIME 5 MINUTES (+ STANDING)
MAKES ¾ CUP

Combine ¾ cup (210g) japanese mayonnaise + 1½ tsp gochujang + ½ tsp rice wine vinegar. Season.

HARISSA AÏOLI

PREP TIME 5 MINUTES **MAKES** 1 CUP

Combine 2 tsp harissa + 1 tsp smoked paprika + 2 tsp lemon juice in a small bowl. Stir ½ cup whole-egg aïoli + ½ cup (140g) sour cream in a second small bowl. Swirl harissa mixture through aïoli mixture.

GREEN GODDESS DRESSING

PREP TIME 10 MINUTES **MAKES** ¾ CUP

Process ¼ cup whole-egg mayonnaise + 2 tbsp sour cream + ¼ cup coarsely chopped flat-leaf parsley + 1 tbsp each coarsely chopped basil and chives + 1 tbsp lemon juice + 2 tbsp water + 1 coarsely chopped anchovy fillet + 1 finely chopped clove garlic until smooth; season.

MEXICAN MAYO

PREP TIME 5 MINUTES **MAKES** ¾ CUP

Process ¾ cup (210g) whole-egg mayonnaise + 1 chilli in adobo sauce (or ½ tsp smoked paprika + ¼ tsp ground chilli) until smooth. Stir in ⅓ cup chopped coriander (cilantro).

THAI FISH CAKES

WITH VERMICELLI HERB SALAD

THAI FISH CAKES & LIME DRESSING

750g (1½lb) skinless firm white fish
fillets, cut into pieces

1 tbsp thai red curry paste

2 tbsp fish sauce

4 kaffir lime leaves, shredded

3 cloves garlic, crushed

⅓ cup thai basil leaves, shredded

½ cup (125ml) olive oil

⅓ cup (80ml) lime juice

1 fresh long red chilli, sliced thinly

VERMICELLI HERB SALAD

100g (3oz) dried brown rice
vermicelli noodles

⅓ cup thai basil leaves

1 medium carrot (120g), shredded

SRIRACHA MAYO

2 tbsp whole-egg mayonnaise

½ tsp sriracha

ASSEMBLY INGREDIENTS

2 baby gem lettuce (romaine) (260g)

4 baby cucumbers (qukes) (120g)

1 brioche roll, halved, toasted

1 medium carrot (120g), shredded

2 tsp olive oil

125g (4oz) microwave brown
and wild rice, heated

2 tsp thai red curry paste

2 kaffir lime leaves, shredded

⅓ cup thai basil leaves

O MEAL PREP

Thai fish cakes & lime dressing Process fish + curry paste
+ 1 tbsp fish sauce + lime leaves + 2 cloves garlic + thai basil leaves
until smooth. Shape mixture into 12 patties. Cook patties in 2 tbsp oil
in a large non-stick frying pan over medium heat for 2 minutes each
side until cooked through.

To make lime dressing, combine remaining oil + remaining fish sauce
+ remaining crushed garlic + lime juice + chilli in a screw-top jar.

Vermicelli herb salad Pour boiling water over noodles and stand
for 5 minutes until softened; drain well. Combine with thai basil
leaves + carrot.

Sriracha mayo Combine mayonnaise + sriracha.

O STORING

Divide thai fish cakes into 4 portions. Divide vermicelli herb salad
into 2 portions. Store lime dressing in a screw-top jar and sriracha
mayo in a container. Refrigerate for up to 4 days.

O ASSEMBLY (SEE PAGE 90)

Meal 1 Thai fish cakes with vermicelli herb salad

Meal 2 Thai fish cake lettuce bowl

Meal 3 Thai fish burger

Meal 4 Thai fish cake fried rice

MEAL 1

THAI FISH CAKES WITH VERMICELLI HERB SALAD

Combine 1 portion vermicelli herb salad with ¼ cup of the lime dressing. Serve with 1 portion reheated thai fish cakes + 1 gem lettuce, shredded + 2 baby cucumbers, cut into batons.

MEAL 2

THAI FISH CAKE LETTUCE BOWL

Combine 1 portion vermicelli herb salad with ¼ cup of the lime dressing. Add 1 portion reheated thai fish cakes, sliced + 1 baby cucumber, chopped + ½ gem lettuce leaves.

MEAL 3

THAI FISH BURGER

Spread brioche base with 1 tbsp sriracha mayo. Top with ½ gem lettuce leaves + ½ shredded carrot + 1 baby cucumber, cut into ribbons + 1 portion reheated thai fish cakes + another 1 tbsp sriracha mayo + brioche top.

MEAL 4

THAI FISH CAKE FRIED RICE

Heat oil in a wok over high heat. Add heated rice + curry paste; cook for 1 minute. Add 1 portion thai fish cakes, diced + ½ shredded carrot + kaffir lime leaves + thai basil leaves; stir until warmed through.

BAKED SALMON & SWEET POTATO
WITH BROCCOLI PESTO

BROCCOLI PESTO

200g (6½oz) broccoli, cut into florets

⅓ cup firmly packed basil leaves

1 small clove garlic, crushed

¼ cup (25g) roasted walnuts

¼ cup (20g) finely grated parmesan

2 tbsp extra virgin olive oil

1 lemon, rind grated finely, then juiced

BAKED SALMON & SWEET POTATO

4 small orange sweet potatoes (1kg)

4 x 150g (4½oz) skinless boneless salmon fillets

ASSEMBLY INGREDIENTS

60g (2oz) baby spinach leaves

⅓ cup (80ml) extra virgin olive oil

¼ cup (20g) finely grated parmesan

lemon wedges, to serve

10 cherry bocconcini (150g), torn

400g (12½oz) can cannellini beans, drained, rinsed

¼ cup (25g) roasted walnuts

⭕ MEAL PREP

Broccoli pesto Blanch broccoli for 1 minute. Process half the broccoli (reserve remaining for meal 4) + basil + garlic + walnuts + parmesan + oil + ½ tsp lemon rind + 1 tbsp lemon juice until smooth. Season.

Baked salmon & sweet potato Preheat oven to 200°C/400°F. Poke holes in sweet potatoes with a skewer; roast on a baking-paper-lined oven tray for 40 minutes until tender.

Meanwhile, press ¼ cup broccoli pesto onto 1 salmon fillet only. Place all salmon fillets on another baking-paper-lined oven tray; season. Bake for the last 7 minutes of sweet potato cooking time until just cooked through.

⭕ STORING

Divide baked salmon and sweet potato, separately, into 4 portions. Store remaining broccoli pesto in a container. Refrigerate for up to 4 days.

⭕ ASSEMBLY (SEE PAGE 94)

Meal 1 Baked salmon & sweet potato with broccoli pesto

Meal 2 Loaded salmon sweet potato

Meal 3 Salmon, pesto & bean salad

Meal 4 Salmon & sweet potato hash

MEAL 1

BAKED SALMON & SWEET POTATO WITH BROCCOLI PESTO

Cut 1 portion sweet potato lengthways into wedges. Serve with reheated pesto-topped baked salmon + 15g spinach dressed with 1 tbsp oil combined with 1 tbsp lemon juice (from broccoli pesto). Sprinkle with 1 tbsp parmesan; season. Serve with 1 lemon wedge.

MEAL 2

LOADED SALMON SWEET POTATO

Slice a cross in the top of 1 portion sweet potato; gently squeeze from bottom to open out. Add 1 portion reheated baked salmon, flaked + 15g spinach + 5 torn bocconcini. Drizzle with 1 tbsp oil combined with 2 tsp lemon juice (from broccoli pesto); season. Top with 2 tbsp broccoli pesto. Serve with 1 lemon wedge.

MEAL 3

SALMON, PESTO & BEAN SALAD

Combine half the beans + 1 portion sweet potato, coarsely chopped + 5 torn bocconcini + 15g spinach + walnuts. Drizzle with 1 tbsp oil combined with 1 tbsp lemon juice (from broccoli pesto) + 1 tsp lemon rind (from broccoli pesto). Season. Add 1 portion reheated baked salmon, flaked. Top salad with 2 tbsp broccoli pesto mixed with 1 tsp water.

MEAL 4

SALMON & SWEET POTATO HASH

Combine 1 portion reheated baked salmon, flaked + remaining beans, crushed + 1 portion sweet potato, mashed + ½ tsp lemon rind (from broccoli pesto) + reserved broccoli (from broccoli pesto) + 15g spinach + 2 tbsp grated parmesan. Heat 1 tbsp oil in a non-stick frying pan. Cook sweet potato mixture for 4 minutes, gently turning and being careful not to break it up; season. Top with 2 tbsp broccoli pesto. Serve with 1 lemon wedge.

PICK YOUR PROTEIN

BEEF

SMOKY BARBECUE STEAK

WITH BRAISED CAPSICUM

SMOKY BARBECUE STEAK

1 tbsp extra virgin olive oil

¼ cup (60ml) barbecue sauce

1½ tsp smoked paprika

4 x 250g (8oz) porterhouse steaks, trimmed, at room temperature

BRAISED CAPSICUM

1 tbsp extra virgin olive oil

1 tsp smoked paprika

3 medium capsicums (bell peppers) (600g), cut into eighths

2 cloves garlic, crushed

2 tsp red wine vinegar

ASSEMBLY INGREDIENTS

1 bunch coriander (cilantro)

¾ cup (210g) greek yoghurt

2 regular wholegrain tortillas, warmed

2 medium avocados (500g)

¾ tsp smoked paprika

400g (12½oz) can black beans, drained (¼ cup liquid reserved), rinsed

100g (3oz) purchased sweet potato chips

2 tsp lime juice

lime cheeks, to serve

⭕ MEAL PREP

Smoky barbecue steak Heat oil in a large heavy-based frying pan over high heat. Combine barbecue sauce + paprika; reserve 1 tbsp of barbecue sauce mixture. Rub steaks with remaining mixture; season. Cook steaks for 3 minutes each side for medium-rare or until cooked to your liking; transfer to a plate. Brush steaks with reserved barbecue sauce mixture; cover loosely with foil to keep warm.

Braised capsicum Heat oil in a clean large frying pan over high heat. Cook paprika + capsicum + garlic, stirring occasionally, for 3 minutes until starting to soften. Add vinegar; cover and cook over medium heat for 4 minutes until softened. Season.

⭕ STORING

Divide smoky barbecue steak and braised capsicum, separately, into 4 portions. Refrigerate for up to 4 days.

⭕ ASSEMBLY (SEE PAGE 100)

Meal 1 Smoky barbecue steak with braised capsicum

Meal 2 Beef & capsicum quesadillas

Meal 3 Cheat's chilli con carne

Meal 4 Smoky beef avocado 'bowls'

Tips Meal 2 can be cooked in a hot sandwich press, if preferred.

For meals 3 and 4, you can carb-it-down by omitting the sweet potato chips and serving in lettuce cups instead.

MEAL 1

SMOKY BARBECUE STEAK WITH BRAISED CAPSICUM

Mix 1 portion braised capsicum + ¼ cup coriander leaves. Serve with 1 portion reheated smoky barbecue steak, sliced + ¼ cup yoghurt.

MEAL 2

BEEF & CAPSICUM QUESADILLAS

Divide 1 portion braised capsicum between tortillas; top with 1 portion reheated barbecue steak, thinly sliced + 2 tbsp coriander leaves. Cook 1 tortilla at a time in a non-stick frying pan over medium heat for 1 minute until golden. Fold to enclose filling; cook, covered, for 1 minute until hot. Serve with ½ avocado, mashed + ¼ cup yoghurt, sprinkled with ¼ tsp paprika.

MEAL 3

CHEAT'S CHILLI CON CARNE

Cook beans + reserved canning liquid + 1 portion braised capsicum + ½ tsp paprika + 2 tbsp water in a small saucepan over medium heat for 5 minutes (reserve a third of the bean mixture for meal 4). Add 1 portion smoky barbecue steak, thinly sliced, to pan; stir until warmed through. Serve with three-quarters of the sweet potato chips + ½ avocado, diced, dressed with lime juice. Top with ¼ cup coriander leaves.

MEAL 4

SMOKY BEEF AVOCADO 'BOWLS'

Top 1 avocado, halved or quartered, with reheated bean mixture (from meal 3) + ¼ cup yoghurt + remaining quarter of the sweet potato chips + 2 tbsp coriander leaves. Serve with 1 portion smoky barbecue steak, thinly sliced + 2 lime cheeks.

MUSTARD RUMP STEAKS

WITH BEETROOT FETTA

ROAST PUMPKIN & ONION

500g (1lb) kent pumpkin, seeds removed, cut into thin wedges

1 medium red onion (170g), cut into wedges

1 tbsp extra virgin olive oil

MUSTARD RUMP STEAKS

1 tbsp wholegrain mustard

1 tbsp extra virgin olive oil

2 tsp red wine vinegar

2 x 500g (1lb) mini rump roasts, at room temperature

BEETROOT FETTA

250g (8oz) vacuum-packed cooked beetroot (beets), drained

50g (1½oz) drained persian fetta (2 tsp marinating oil reserved)

ASSEMBLY INGREDIENTS

120g (4oz) baby spinach and beetroot (beets) leaf salad mix

1½ tbsp extra virgin olive oil

1 tbsp red wine vinegar

200g (9½oz) drained persian fetta

1 seeded bread roll, halved, warmed

1 tsp wholegrain mustard

125g (4oz) can chickpeas (garbanzo beans), drained, rinsed

½ bunch mint

250g (8oz) vacuum-packed cooked beetroot (beets), drained

½ cup (100g) pearl couscous

⭕ MEAL PREP

Roast pumpkin & onion Preheat oven to at 220°C/425°F. Combine pumpkin + onion + oil on a baking-paper-lined oven tray; season. Roast for 20 minutes until tender and caramelised.

Mustard rump steaks Meanwhile, combine mustard + oil + vinegar; rub over mini roasts. Season. Cook on oiled grill plate over medium-high heat for 3 minutes each side or until cooked to your liking. Cover; rest for 10 minutes.

Beetroot fetta Meanwhile, blend beetroot + fetta + marinating oil + 2 tbsp water until smooth; season. Heat in a small saucepan over low heat, stirring, for 3 minutes until warmed through.

⭕ STORING

Divide roast pumpkin & onion and mustard rump steaks, separately, into 4 portions. Divide beetroot fetta into 3 portions. Refrigerate for up to 4 days.

⭕ ASSEMBLY (SEE PAGE 104)

Meal 1 Mustard rump steak with beetroot fetta

Meal 2 Mustard steak sandwich

Meal 3 Mustard beef, pumpkin & chickpea salad

Meal 4 Pearl couscous, beef & beetroot salad

MEAL 1

MUSTARD RUMP STEAKS WITH BEETROOT FETTA

Serve 1 portion reheated mustard rump steak, thinly sliced + 1 portion roast pumpkin & onion + 1 portion beetroot fetta + 40g (1½oz) salad leaves dressed with 2 tsp oil combined with 1 tsp vinegar. Add 50g (1½oz) fetta, cubed.

MEAL 2

MUSTARD STEAK SANDWICH

Spread bread roll base with 1 portion beetroot fetta. Spread roll top with mustard. Top base with 40g (1½oz) salad leaves dressed with 2 tsp oil combined with 1 tsp vinegar + 1 portion roast pumpkin & onion + 1 portion reheated mustard rump steak, thinly sliced + 50g (1½oz) fetta, crumbled.

MEAL 3

MUSTARD BEEF, PUMPKIN & CHICKPEA SALAD

Combine 2 tsp oil + 1 tsp vinegar; season. Add 1 portion reheated mustard rump steak, thinly sliced + 1 portion roast pumpkin & onion + chickpeas + 40g (1½oz) salad leaves + ¼ cup mint leaves + 50g (1½oz) fetta, crumbled + 125g (4oz) beetroot, quartered.

MEAL 4

PEARL COUSCOUS, BEEF & BEETROOT SALAD

Cook couscous in pan of boiling salted water for 6 minutes until tender; drain. Combine couscous + 1 portion beetroot fetta + 1 tsp vinegar; stir to coat. Add 1 portion roast pumpkin & onion + 125g (4oz) beetroot, quartered + 50g (1½oz) fetta, crumbled + 2 tbsp mint leaves. Serve with 1 portion reheated mustard rump steak, thinly sliced.

COLESLAW THREE WAYS

PREP & COOK TIME 10 MINUTES
MAKES 3 PORTIONS

BASIC COLESLAW MIXTURE Combine 600g (1¼lb)
packet fine-cut coleslaw + 2 medium carrots, cut into
matchsticks + 1 small red apple, cut into matchsticks
+ 6 thinly sliced green onions (scallions) + ⅓ cup
finely chopped flat-leaf parsley in a bowl. Cover;
refrigerate until needed.

Meal 1: Classic dressing Combine ⅓ cup whole-egg mayonnaise + 2 tbsp white wine vinegar + a third basic coleslaw mixture (recipe, left).

Meal 2: Mustardy vinaigrette Combine ⅓ cup extra virgin olive oil + 2 tbsp white wine vinegar + 1 tbsp dijon mustard + 2 tsp finely grated lemon rind + a third basic coleslaw mixture (recipe, left).

Meal 3: Kimchi crunch dressing Combine ¼ cup (25g) finely shredded kimchi + 1 tbsp rice wine vinegar + 1 tbsp honey + 1 tbsp extra virgin olive oil + 1 tbsp sesame oil + a third basic coleslaw mixture (recipe, left). Serve scattered with 2 tbsp white sesame seeds + ½ cup roasted unsalted cashews.

BULGOGI BEEF

BULGOGI BEEF & NOODLES

⅓ cup (80ml) soy sauce

2 tsp caster (superfine) sugar

1 clove garlic, crushed

1 tsp finely grated fresh ginger

4 green onions (scallions), chopped finely

2 tbsp olive oil

½ tsp sesame oil

500g (1lb) piece beef eye fillet, sliced very thinly

2 x 100g (3oz) packets dried sweet potato noodles

ASSEMBLY INGREDIENTS

4 gem lettuce leaves

1 small red capsicum (bell pepper) (150g), sliced thinly

4 green onions (scallions), sliced thinly

1 tbsp olive oil

1½ cups (300g) kimchi

1 bunch baby buk choy (160g), quartered lengthways

200g (6½oz) asian mixed mushrooms, sliced

1 cup (250ml) beef stock

○ MEAL PREP

Bulgogi beef & noodles Combine soy sauce + sugar + garlic + ginger + green onions + oils. Add ¼ cup dressing to beef and toss to coat (reserve remaining dressing for meals). Refrigerate beef for 20 minutes to marinate. Drain; discard marinade. Cook beef on a hot oiled chargrill plate over high heat for 30 seconds each side.

Cook noodles following packet directions; drain.

○ STORING

Divide bulgogi beef and noodles, separately, into 4 portions. Refrigerate for up to 4 days.

○ ASSEMBLY (SEE PAGE 110)

Meal 1 Bulgogi beef

Meal 2 Kimchi beef noodle stir-fry

Meal 3 Bulgogi beef bowl

Meal 4 Bulgogi beef stew

MEAL 1

BULGOGI BEEF

Serve 4 lettuce leaves + 1 portion noodles tossed with 1 tbsp of the reserved dressing (from bulgogi beef & noodles) + 1 portion reheated bulgogi beef + ½ sliced capsicum. Drizzle with another 1 tbsp reserved dressing (from bulgogi beef & noodles). Top with 1 thinly sliced green onion.

MEAL 2

KIMCHI BEEF NOODLE STIR-FRY

Heat 2 tsp oil in a wok over high heat. Cook 1 thinly sliced green onion + ½ sliced capsicum for 2 minutes until softened. Add 1 cup kimchi + 1 portion noodles tossed with 1 tbsp reserved dressing (from bulgogi beef & noodles) + 1 portion bulgogi beef; stir-fry for 2 minutes until warmed through.

MEAL 3

BULGOGI BEEF BOWL

Combine 1 portion noodles tossed with 1 tbsp reserved dressing (from bulgogi beef & noodles). Add 1 portion reheated bulgogi beef + ½ cup kimchi + 1 baby buk choy, blanched + 1 tbsp reserved dressing (from bulgogi beef & noodles) + 1 thinly sliced green onion.

MEAL 4

BULGOGI BEEF STEW

Heat 2 tsp oil in a small saucepan. Cook sliced mushrooms + 1 thinly sliced green onion for 2 minutes. Add stock + 2 baby buk choy, sliced; bring to a simmer. Add 1 portion bulgogi beef + 1 portion noodles + 1 tbsp reserved dressing (from bulgogi beef & noodles); cook for 2 minutes until warmed through.

MEXICAN ROAST BEEF DINNER

MEXICAN ROAST BEEF & VEGETABLES

1 tbsp extra virgin olive oil

500g (1lb) beef eye fillet

35g (1oz) packet taco seasoning mix

2 tbsp coarsely chopped coriander (cilantro) roots and stems

500g (1lb) baby (chat) potatoes, halved

350g (11oz) vine sweet mini capsicums (bell peppers)

1 medium red onion (170g), quartered

400g (12½oz) can black beans, drained, rinsed

400g (12½oz) bottle arrabbiata pasta sauce

ASSEMBLY INGREDIENTS

30g (1oz) baby rocket (arugula)

1½ tbsp extra virgin olive oil

1 medium avocado (250g)

lime wedges or cheeks, to serve

½ cup coriander (cilantro) leaves

250g (8oz) packet microwave mexican rice, heated

1 tbsp coarsely chopped coriander (cilantro) roots and stems

1 cup (250ml) beef stock

1 tbsp sour cream

1 small white corn wrap

⅓ cup (35g) pizza cheese

2 tsp lime juice

⭘ MEAL PREP

Mexican roast beef & vegetables Preheat oven to 200°C/400°F. Rub oil over beef; sprinkle with 2 tbsp taco seasoning (reserve remaining for meals 2 and 3) + coriander roots and stems. Place potatoes + capsicums + 3 onion quarters (reserve remaining quarter for meal 4) + beans + all but ¼ cup pasta sauce (reserve for meal 4) in a roasting pan; top with beef. Roast for 25 minutes until beef is cooked to medium. Remove meat; cover loosely and stand. Increase oven to 220°C/425°F; cook vegetables for a further 10 minutes until potato is golden.

⭘ STORING

Divide mexican roast beef into 4 portions. Divide roast vegetables into 3 portions. Refrigerate for up to 4 days.

⭘ ASSEMBLY (SEE PAGE 114)

Meal 1 Mexican roast beef dinner

Meal 2 Mexican beef rice pilaf

Meal 3 Mexican beef & bean soup

Meal 4 Mexican beef pizza

MEAL 1

MEXICAN ROAST BEEF DINNER

Serve 1 portion reheated mexican roast beef, thickly sliced + 1 portion roast vegetables + rocket dressed with 1 tsp oil + ½ avocado, diced + 1 lime wedge. Season.

MEAL 2

MEXICAN BEEF RICE PILAF

Heat 2 tsp oil in a wok. Add 2 tsp reserved taco seasoning (from mexican roast beef & vegetables) + 1 tbsp coriander leaves; cook for 1 minute. Add heated rice + 1 portion roast vegetables, chopped + 1 portion mexican roast beef, thinly sliced; stir-fry for 1 minute until warmed through. Top with 2 tbsp coriander leaves. Serve with 1 lime wedge.

MEAL 3

MEXICAN BEEF & BEAN SOUP

Heat 2 tsp oil in a saucepan. Add 2 tsp taco seasoning (from mexican roast beef & vegetables) + chopped coriander root and stems; cook for 1 minute. Add 1 portion roast vegetables, chopped + 1 portion mexican roast beef, thinly sliced + stock; simmer for 2 minutes until warmed through. Top with sour cream + 2 tbsp coriander leaves. Serve with 1 lime cheek.

MEAL 4

MEXICAN BEEF PIZZA

Preheat oven to 200°C/400°F, with a foil-lined tray inside, for 5 minutes. Bake wrap on tray for 10 minutes until crisp. Spread reserved ¼ cup pasta sauce (from mexican roast beef & vegetables) over wrap. Top with reserved thinly sliced onion quarter (from mexican roast beef & vegetables) + 1 portion mexican roast beef, thinly sliced + cheese. Cook pizza for 5 minutes until golden. Top with ½ avocado mashed with lime juice + 1 tbsp coriander leaves. Serve with 1 lime wedge.

LOADED VEGIE REUBEN BEEF PATTIES

REUBEN BEEF PATTIES

500g (1lb) minced (ground) beef

1 large carrot (180g), shredded

1 medium zucchini (240g), grated

1 large lemon, rind grated finely, then juiced

2 cloves garlic, crushed

2 tbsp dijonnaise

4 slices swiss cheese (90g)

ASSEMBLY INGREDIENTS

3 slices light rye bread (135g)

¼ cup (70g) dijonnaise

½ butter (boston) lettuce (100g)

½ cup (90g) purchased red sauerkraut

⅓ cup (80g) sour cream

¼ cup (60ml) extra virgin olive oil

3 large flat mushrooms (240g)

3 tsp tomato paste

2 tsp worcestershire sauce

1 medium zucchini (240g), spiralised

⊙ MEAL PREP

Reuben beef patties Process mince + 100g (3oz) carrot (reserve remaining for meals 2 and 4) + zucchini + 2 tsp finely grated lemon rind (reserve juice for meal 2) + garlic + dijonnaise until well combined; season. Shape mixture into four patties. Heat an oiled chargrill plate over high heat; cook patties for 5 minutes each side until cooked through. Melt 1 slice cheese on each pattie for the last 1 minute of cooking time.

⊙ STORING

Divide reuben beef patties into 4 portions. Refrigerate for up to 4 days.

⊙ ASSEMBLY (SEE PAGE 118)

Meal 1 Reuben beef pattie sandwich

Meal 2 Reuben beef pattie salad

Meal 3 Reuben beef pattie stroganoff

Meal 4 Mushroom reuben beef pattie 'burger'

MEAL 1

REUBEN BEEF PATTIE SANDWICH

Spread 1 slice toasted rye bread with 1 tbsp dijonnaise. Top with 2 lettuce leaves + 1 portion reheated reuben beef pattie + 2 tbsp sauerkraut; season. Top with 1 slice rye bread, toasted.

MEAL 2

REUBEN BEEF PATTIE SALAD

Combine 1 tbsp sour cream + 1 tbsp dijonnaise + 1 tsp reserved lemon juice (from reuben beef patties). Serve ¼ lettuce, cut into wedges + 1 portion reheated reuben beef pattie, thickly sliced + 1 tbsp reserved grated carrot (from reuben beef patties) + ¼ cup sauerkraut + 1 slice rye bread, toasted and broken into pieces; season. Drizzle with dijonnaise dressing.

MEAL 3

REUBEN BEEF PATTIE STROGANOFF

Heat 1 tbsp oil in a non-stick frying pan; cook 1 mushroom, sliced, for 3 minutes until golden. Add tomato paste + worcestershire sauce; cook for 1 minute. Add 2 tbsp sour cream; stir to warm through. Serve with warmed zucchini noodles + 1 portion reheated reuben beef pattie, thickly sliced; season.

MEAL 4

MUSHROOM REUBEN BEEF PATTIE 'BURGER'

Heat 2 tbsp oil in a frying pan over medium heat; cook 2 whole mushrooms for 5 minutes, turning halfway through cooking time, until tender. Top 1 mushroom with 2 large lettuce leaves + 1 portion reheated reuben beef pattie + 1 tbsp dijonnaise mixed with 1 tbsp sour cream. Top with remaining whole mushroom. Serve with 1 tbsp reserved grated carrot (from reuben beef patties) + 1 tbsp sauerkraut; season.

HOISIN BEEF
WITH QUICKLED CUCUMBERS

HOISIN BEEF & GAI LAN

½ cup (125ml) hoisin sauce

2 tsp sambal oelek

4 x 250g (8oz) porterhouse steaks, trimmed, at room temperature

1 tbsp vegetable oil

1 bunch gai lan (500g), trimmed, cut crossways into thirds

QUICKLED CUCUMBERS

250g (8oz) baby cucumbers (qukes)

⅓ cup (80ml) rice wine vinegar

1 tsp caster (superfine) sugar

2 tsp white sesame seeds, toasted

ASSEMBLY INGREDIENTS

2 x 400g (12½oz) packets konjac noodles, heated

1 cup (250ml) beef stock

¼ cup (60ml) hoisin sauce

3 tsp sambal oelek

1¼ cups (100g) bean sprouts

¼ cup thai basil leaves

1½ tsp white sesame seeds, toasted

2 wholemeal roti (120g), warmed

⭘ MEAL PREP

Hoisin beef & gai lan Combine hoisin sauce + sambal oelek; reserve 2 tablespoons hoisin mixture. Rub remaining hoisin mixture over steaks. Heat oil in a large non-stick frying pan over medium-high heat; cook steaks for 3 minutes each side for medium or until cooked to your liking. Transfer to a plate. Brush with the reserved hoisin mixture. Cover with foil; rest.

Cook gai lan stems in a medium saucepan of salted boiling water for 2 minutes until just tender. Add leaves; cook for a further 1 minute or until tender. Drain.

Quickled cucumbers Press each cucumber lightly with the flat side of a large knife to crack lightly. Combine cucumbers, vinegar, sugar and sesame seeds in a bowl.

⭘ STORING

Divide hoisin beef into 4 portions. Divide quickled cucumbers into 3 portions. Divide gai lan into 2 portions. Refrigerate for up to 4 days.

⭘ ASSEMBLY (SEE PAGE 122)

Meal 1 Hoisin beef with quickled cucumbers

Meal 2 No-carb pho

Meal 3 Chilli beef noodles

Meal 4 Mushu beef wraps

MEAL 1

HOISIN BEEF WITH QUICKLED CUCUMBERS

Serve 1 portion reheated hoisin beef
+ any resting beef juices + 1 portion gai lan
+ half a packet heated noodles + 1 portion
quickled cucumbers in a bowl.

MEAL 2

NO-CARB PHO

Bring stock + 1 cup water to the boil in a small
saucepan. Add half a packet heated noodles
+ 1 portion hoisin beef, thinly sliced + 1 portion
gai lan; cook for 1 minute to heat through.
Season. Add 2 tsp each hoisin sauce and
sambal oelek. Top with ½ cup bean sprouts
+ thai basil leaves.

MEAL 3

CHILLI BEEF NOODLES

Cook 1 portion hoisin beef, sliced + 1 packet
heated noodles + ½ cup bean sprouts + 1 tsp each
hoisin sauce and sambal oelek in an oiled large
non-stick frying pan over high heat for 3 minutes
until warmed through. Top with 1 tsp sesame seeds
+ 1 portion quickled cucumbers, chopped.

MEAL 4

MUSHU BEEF WRAPS

Spread 1 tbsp hoisin sauce on each roti.
Top with 1 portion hoisin beef, sliced
+ 1 portion quickled cucumbers, chopped
+ ¼ cup bean sprouts + ½ tsp sesame seeds.

TEXAN BEEF MEATLOAF

TEXAN BEEF MEATLOAF

1kg (2lb) minced (ground) beef

400g (12½oz) can red kidney beans,
drained, rinsed

35g (1oz) sachet taco seasoning mix

¾ cup (180ml) taco sauce

½ cup finely chopped coriander
(cilantro) leaves and stems

2 eggs

**SWEET POTATO WEDGES
& ROAST TOMATOES**

2 small orange sweet potatoes (500g),
cut into wedges

2 tbsp extra virgin olive oil

200g (6½oz) cherry truss tomatoes

ASSEMBLY INGREDIENTS

½ medium avocado (125g)

120g (4oz) baby spinach and
rocket salad mix

2 tbsp extra virgin olive oil

1 medium lemon, juiced

2 taco shells (20g), warmed

½ cup (60g) grated tasty cheese

50g (1½oz) cherry truss tomatoes

1 tbsp sour cream

¼ cup coriander (cilantro) leaves

1 egg

⅓ cup (80ml) taco sauce

1 medium red capsicum (bell pepper)
(200g), halved, seeded

O MEAL PREP

Texan beef meatloaf Preheat oven to 180°C/350°F. Mix together mince + beans + seasoning + ½ cup taco sauce + coriander + eggs until well combined. Press into a greased 25.5cm x 13cm (10¼in x 5¼in), 8cm (3¼in) deep loaf pan. Pour over remaining ¼ cup taco sauce. Bake for 45 minutes until lightly golden and cooked through.

Sweet potato wedges & roast tomatoes Meanwhile, combine sweet potato + oil; season. Bake on a baking-paper-lined oven tray for 20 minutes. Add tomatoes; roast for a further 10 minutes.

O STORING

Divide texan beef meatloaf into 4 portions. Divide sweet potato wedges and roast tomatoes, separately, into 2 portions. Refrigerate for up to 4 days.

O ASSEMBLY (SEE PAGE 126)

Meal 1 Texan beef meatloaf

Meal 2 Loaded texan beef tacos

Meal 3 Meatloaf & egg fry-up

Meal 4 Texan stuffed capsicum

MEAL 1

TEXAN BEEF MEATLOAF

Serve 1 portion reheated texan beef meatloaf,
sliced + 1 portion sweet potato wedges
+ 1 portion roast tomatoes. Add ¼ avocado,
cut into wedges + 40g (1½oz) salad leaves
dressed with 1 tbsp oil + 2 tsp lemon juice.

MEAL 2

LOADED TEXAN BEEF TACOS

Fill taco shells with 40g (1½oz) salad leaves
+ 1 portion reheated texan beef meatloaf, sliced
+ ¼ cup cheese + fresh cherry tomatoes, halved
+ ¼ avocado mashed with 1 tbsp lemon juice.
Top with sour cream + 2 tbsp coriander leaves.

MEAL 3

MEATLOAF & EGG FRY-UP

Fry egg in an oiled small non-stick frying pan
until cooked to your liking; transfer to a plate.
Cook 1 portion chopped sweet potato wedges
+ 2 tbsp taco sauce for 2 minutes until warmed
through; add to plate. Fry 1 portion texan beef
meatloaf, sliced, for 2 minutes each side until
golden. Serve meatloaf with sweet potato mixture
+ 1 portion roast tomatoes. Top with fried egg
+ 2 tbsp coriander leaves.

MEAL 4

TEXAN STUFFED CAPSICUM

Preheat oven to 180°C/350°F. Chop 1 portion
texan beef meatloaf; divide between
capsicum halves. Top with 2 tbsp taco sauce
+ ¼ cup cheese. Bake for 25 minutes until
cheese melts and capsicum softens.
Serve with 40g (1½oz) salad leaves dressed
with 1 tbsp olive oil + 2 tsp lemon juice.

PICK YOUR PROTEIN

MEAT FREE

STICKY GLAZED TOFU
WITH CHILLI-LIME BROCCOLINI

STICKY GLAZED TOFU & CAPSICUM

500g (1lb) firm tofu, cut into
1.5cm (¾in) thick slices

⅓ cup (80ml) kecap manis

2 tbsp olive oil

350g (11oz) vine sweet mini capsicums
(bell peppers), halved

CHILLI-LIME BROCCOLINI

1½ tbsp olive oil

2 bunches broccolini (350g), trimmed

1 fresh long green chilli, chopped finely

1 clove garlic, chopped finely

1 tsp finely grated lime rind

1½ tbsp lime juice

ASSEMBLY INGREDIENTS

250g (8oz) microwave brown
and wild rice, heated

4 green onions (scallions), shredded

lime cheeks or wedges, to serve

1 cup (200g) frozen shelled edamame
(soy beans), boiled, steamed
or microwaved

1 tsp olive oil

250g (8oz) cherry tomatoes, halved

2 tbsp hoisin sauce

1 brioche roll

⭕ MEAL PREP

Sticky glazed tofu & capsicum Combine tofu + kecap manis. Heat oil in a large non-stick frying pan over medium heat. Cook drained tofu slices for 2 minutes each side until caramelised; remove from pan. Add capsicum + any remaining kecap manis marinade + ¼ cup water. Cook, stirring, for 4 minutes until softened and saucy. Return tofu slices to pan.

Chilli-lime broccolini Heat 2 tsp oil in a cleaned frying pan; cook broccolini over high heat for 2 minutes on each side until just tender. Transfer to a bowl; add 1 tbsp oil + chilli + garlic + lime rind + lime juice. Season to taste.

⭕ STORING

Divide sticky glazed tofu & capsicum into 4 portions. Divide chilli-lime broccolini into 3 portions. Refrigerate for up to 4 days.

⭕ ASSEMBLY (SEE PAGE 132)

Meal 1 Sticky glazed tofu with chilli-lime broccolini

Meal 2 Sticky glazed tofu with broccolini-edamame smash

Meal 3 Sticky glazed tofu fried rice

Meal 4 Sticky glazed tofu non-carne slider

MEAL 1

STICKY GLAZED TOFU WITH CHILLI-LIME BROCCOLINI

Serve 1 portion reheated sticky glazed tofu & capsicum + 1 portion chilli-lime broccolini + 125g (4oz) heated rice. Top with 1 shredded green onion. Serve with 1 lime cheek.

MEAL 2

STICKY GLAZED TOFU WITH BROCCOLINI-EDAMAME SMASH

Puree 1 portion chilli-lime broccolini + ½ cup edamame; season. Serve with 1 portion reheated sticky glazed tofu & capsicum. Top with 1 shredded green onion.

MEAL 3

STICKY GLAZED TOFU FRIED RICE

Coarsely chop 1 portion sticky glazed tofu & capsicum + 1 portion chilli-lime broccolini. Heat oil in a non-stick frying pan over high heat. Cook tofu mixture + broccolini + 125g (4oz) heated rice + ¼ cup edamame, stirring, for 3 minutes until hot. Top with 1 shredded green onion. Serve with 125g (4oz) cherry tomatoes + 1 lime wedge.

MEAL 4

STICKY GLAZED TOFU NON-CARNE SLIDER

Cook 1 portion sticky glazed tofu & capsicum + hoisin sauce + 125g (4oz) cherry tomatoes + ¼ cup water in a saucepan over medium heat for 10 minutes until hot and thickened. Top bun base with tofu mixture + ¼ cup edamame + 1 shredded green onion + roll top.

TOFU MUSHROOM PATTIES
WITH ASIAN SLAW

TOFU MUSHROOM PATTIES

300g (9½oz) firm tofu, patted dry, grated coarsely

150g (4½oz) button mushrooms, chopped coarsely

½ cup finely chopped coriander (cilantro) leaves and stems

1 clove garlic, crushed

4 kaffir lime leaves, shredded

1 tbsp vegan green curry paste

2½ cups (250g) wholegrain breadcrumbs

1 egg

2 tbsp extra virgin olive oil

ASIAN SLAW

¼ cup (60ml) extra virgin olive oil

¼ cup (60ml) lime juice

2 kaffir lime leaves, shredded

1 clove garlic, crushed

300g (9½oz) bag asian-style coleslaw

ASSEMBLY INGREDIENTS

1 small iceberg lettuce (300g)

250g (8oz) cherry tomatoes, halved

1 small avocado (200g)

½ cup (150g) japanese mayonnaise

3 tsp sriracha sauce

¼ cup coriander (cilantro) leaves

lime cheeks, to serve

1 small baguette or ficelle

1 tbsp roasted cashews

125g (4oz) microwave brown rice, heated

1 soft-boiled egg (see page 183)

O MEAL PREP

Tofu mushroom patties Process tofu + mushrooms + coriander + garlic + lime leaves + curry paste + breadcrumbs + egg until mixture comes together. Shape mixture into four patties. Cover; refrigerate for 20 minutes to firm. Heat oil in a non-stick frying pan over medium heat; cook patties for 5 minutes on each side until golden.

Asian slaw Combine oil + lime juice + lime leaves + garlic in a screw-top jar. Combine coleslaw + ⅓ cup dressing (reserve remaining dressing for meal 4).

O STORING

Divide tofu mushroom patties into 4 portions. Divide asian slaw into 3 portions. Store remaining dressing in a screw-top jar. Refrigerate for up to 4 days.

O ASSEMBLY (SEE PAGE 136)

Meal 1 Tofu mushroom patties with asian slaw

Meal 2 Tofu mushroom pattie banh mi

Meal 3 Tofu mushroom pattie lettuce 'burger'

Meal 4 Tofu mushroom burger power bowl

MEAL 1

TOFU MUSHROOM PATTIES WITH ASIAN SLAW

Combine 1 portion asian slaw + 1 lettuce leaf, shredded. Serve with 1 portion reheated tofu mushroom pattie, halved + a quarter of the cherry tomatoes + ½ avocado, cut into wedges + 2 tbsp mayonnaise mixed with 1 tsp sriracha + 1 tbsp coriander leaves + 1 lime cheek.

MEAL 2

TOFU MUSHROOM PATTIE BANH MI

Spread 2 tbsp mayonnaise mixed with 1 tsp sriracha over base and top of baguette. Top base with 1 lettuce leaf, torn + 1 portion reheated tofu mushroom pattie, sliced + 1 portion asian slaw + a quarter of the cherry tomatoes + 1 tbsp coriander leaves.

MEAL 3

TOFU MUSHROOM PATTIE LETTUCE 'BURGER'

Spoon 1 portion asian slaw into 1 lettuce cup. Top with 1 portion reheated tofu mushroom pattie + 2 tbsp mayonnaise mixed with 1 tsp sriracha + a quarter of the cherry tomatoes + another lettuce cup as the 'burger' lid.

MEAL 4

TOFU MUSHROOM BURGER POWER BOWL

Combine 2 tbsp mayonnaise + 1 tbsp of the reserved dressing (from asian slaw). Combine ¼ iceberg lettuce, cut into a wedge + a quarter of the cherry tomatoes + ½ avocado, chopped; spoon over mayonnaise mixture. Serve with 1 portion reheated tofu mushroom pattie, quartered + cashews + heated rice mixed with 1 tbsp of the reserved dressing (from asian slaw) + soft-boiled egg, halved. Top with 1 tbsp coriander leaves. Serve with 1 lime cheek.

MEGA VEGIE & HALOUMI FRITTATA

MEGA VEGIE & HALOUMI FRITTATA

1 tbsp extra virgin olive oil

400g (12½oz) packet fresh
stir-fry vegetables

400g (12½oz) can chickpeas
(garbanzo beans), drained, rinsed

2 cloves garlic, crushed

3 tsp ground cumin

200g (6½oz) firm ricotta, crumbled

10 eggs, beaten lightly

310g (10oz) jar roasted red capsicum
(bell peppers) strips, drained

115g (3½oz) haloumi, grated

ROAST MUSHROOMS

6 flat mushrooms (375g)

1½ tbsp extra virgin olive oil

LEMON DRESSING

2 tbsp extra virgin olive oil

1 large lemon, rind grated finely,
then juiced

1 clove garlic, crushed

ASSEMBLY INGREDIENTS

60g (2oz) rocket (arugula)

2 tbsp pesto (see page 50)

110g (3½oz) haloumi, cut into 2 slices

2 tsp extra virgin olive oil

1 egg, beaten lightly

60g (2oz) piece parmesan

⬤ MEAL PREP

Mega vegie & haloumi frittata Preheat oven to 200°C/400°F. Grease and line a 20cm x 30cm (8in x 12in) lamington pan with baking paper, extending over long sides. Heat oil in a large non-stick frying pan over medium heat. Add vegetables + chickpeas + garlic + cumin. Cook, stirring, for 2 minutes. Season. Transfer to lined pan. Top with ricotta + egg + ½ cup capsicum strips (reserve remaining for meals 1, 2 and 3) + haloumi. Bake frittata for 25 minutes until frittata is set and golden. Cut frittata into four pieces.

Roast mushrooms Meanwhile, place mushrooms on a baking-paper-lined oven tray; drizzle with oil and season. Bake for 25 minutes.

Lemon dressing Combine oil + 1 tsp grated lemon rind + 2 tbsp lemon juice + garlic in a screw-top jar.

⬤ STORING

Divide vegie & haloumi frittata into 4 portions. Store roast mushrooms in a container. Store lemon dressing in screw-top jar. Refrigerate for up to 4 days.

⬤ ASSEMBLY (SEE PAGE 140)

Meal 1 Mega vegie & haloumi frittata

Meal 2 Frittata 'crouton' salad

Meal 3 Frittata stack with haloumi & mushrooms

Meal 4 Loaded frittata & haloumi finger 'sandwiches'

MEAL 1

MEGA VEGIE & HALOUMI FRITTATA

Serve 1 portion reheated vegie & haloumi frittata + 2 roast mushrooms, halved + ¼ cup capsicum strips + 15g (½oz) rocket. Mix 1 tbsp pesto + 1 tbsp of the lemon dressing; drizzle over frittata and salad.

MEAL 2

FRITTATA 'CROUTON' SALAD

Pan-fry 1 haloumi slice in 1 tsp oil in a non-stick frying pan over medium-high heat for 1 minute each side until golden. Cut 1 portion vegie & haloumi frittata into 3cm (1¼in) cubes; coat in egg + 45g (1½oz) parmesan, finely grated. Grill coated frittata on a foil-lined tray under a hot grill for 1 minute each side until golden. Serve with pan-fried haloumi + 15g (½oz) rocket + 1 roast mushroom, sliced + ¼ cup capsicum strips, dressed with 1 tbsp of the lemon dressing.

MEAL 3

FRITTATA STACK WITH HALOUMI & MUSHROOMS

Pan-fry 1 haloumi slice in 1 tsp oil in a non-stick frying pan over medium-high heat for 1 minute each side until golden. Serve 1 portion reheated vegie & haloumi frittata + pan-fried haloumi with 15g (½oz) rocket + 3 roast mushrooms, sliced + ¼ cup capsicum strips, dressed with 1 tbsp pesto.

MEAL 4

LOADED FRITTATA & HALOUMI FINGER 'SANDWICHES'

Serve 1 portion reheated vegie & haloumi frittata, cut into thick slices + 15g (½oz) rocket dressed with 1 tbsp of the lemon dressing and sprinkled with 15g (½oz) parmesan, shaved.

MEXICAN BEANS BOWL

TOSTADA BOWL & CHIPS

2 jumbo wholegrain tortillas

extra virgin olive oil

MEXICAN BEANS

3 tsp mexican seasoning

3 x 400g (12½oz) cans four-bean mix, drained, rinsed

400g (12½oz) jar arrabbiata pasta sauce

ASSEMBLY INGREDIENTS

60g (2oz) mixed salad leaves

1½ small avocados (300g)

1 buffalo mozzarella (130g), torn

½ cup coriander (cilantro) leaves

1 tbsp extra virgin olive oil

1 tsp mexican seasoning

¾ cup (210g) greek yoghurt

3 tsp tahini

2 eggs

1 jumbo wholegrain tortilla

⬤ MEAL PREP

Tostada bowl & chips Preheat oven to 180°C/350°F. Cut an 8cm (3¼in) wedge from 1 tortilla. Brush tortilla and wedge on both sides with oil. Wrap tortilla around exterior of an ovenproof bowl, about 16cm (6½in) in diameter, domed-side up; slightly overlap cut edges to form the shape of the bowl. Bake for 6 minutes. Carefully transfer tortilla only, domed-side up, to a baking-paper-lined oven tray with the wedge; bake for a further 6 minutes until golden. The tortilla bowl (tostada) will crisp as it cools.

For tortilla chips, cut remaining tortilla into 8 wedges; brush with oil. Bake for 4 minutes on a baking-paper-lined tray until golden; cool.

Mexican beans Meanwhile, bring mexican seasoning + beans + pasta sauce + ½ cup water to a simmer in a frying pan over medium heat. Cook, stirring, for 4 minutes until reduced slightly; season to taste.

⬤ STORING

Store tostada bowl and tostada chips at room temperature in a container. Divide mexican beans into 4 portions and refrigerate for up to 4 days.

⬤ ASSEMBLY (SEE PAGE 144)

Meal 1 Mexican beans bowl

Meal 2 Middle eastern 'nachos'

Meal 3 Mexican pot pie

Meal 4 Huevos rancheros

MEAL 1

MEXICAN BEANS BOWL

Serve 1 portion reheated mexican beans
+ 30g (1oz) salad leaves + ½ avocado, sliced
+ ½ torn mozzarella in the tostada bowl.
Top with a quarter of the coriander leaves.

MEAL 2

MIDDLE EASTERN 'NACHOS'

Heat 2 tsp oil + mexican seasoning + 1 portion
mexican beans in a small saucepan over
high heat until warmed through. Combine
¼ cup yoghurt + tahini; season. Serve
bean mixture + tahini yoghurt + tostada chips
+ ½ avocado, mashed. Top with a quarter of
the coriander leaves.

MEAL 3

MEXICAN POT PIE

Whisk ½ cup yoghurt + 1 egg until combined;
season. Place 1 portion mexican beans in a
1½-cup ovenproof dish. Top with yoghurt mixture.
Bake for 12 minutes until light golden. Top with
30g (1oz) salad leaves + a quarter of the
coriander leaves.

MEAL 4

HUEVOS RANCHEROS

Fry 1 egg in an oiled small non-stick frying pan
over high heat until cooked to your liking.
Serve 1 portion reheated mexican beans
+ 1 warmed fresh tortilla + ½ avocado, diced
+ ½ torn mozzarella + fried egg. Top with a
quarter of the coriander leaves.

MEAL TOPPERS

Combine all ingredients, then season with sea salt and black pepper to taste.

SUPER SEED CRUNCH

PREP & COOK TIME 10 MINUTES MAKES 1¼ CUPS

Heat 2 tbsp olive oil in a small non-stick frying pan over medium heat. Add ⅓ cup coarsely chopped natural almonds + ¼ cup pepitas (pumpkin seed kernels) + 2 tbsp sunflower seeds; cook, stirring, for 1 minute. Add 1 tbsp each coriander seeds + black sesame seeds; cook, stirring, for a further 2 minutes until toasted lightly. Cool.

SESAME & SEAWEED SPRINKLE

PREP & COOK TIME 15 MINUTES MAKES 1¼ CUPS

Using kitchen scissors, snip 2 nori (seaweed) sheets into fine strips. Place ¼ cup sesame seeds + 1 tsp sea salt flakes in a small frying pan; stir constantly over medium heat for 5 minutes until golden. Add nori strips; stir for a further 1 minute until lightly toasted. Transfer to a bowl; stir in ¼ cup fried asian shallots + 1 tsp dried chilli flakes.

LEMON, GARLIC & CHILLI CRUMBS

PREP & COOK TIME 15 MINUTES MAKES 1½ CUPS

Heat 40g (1½oz) butter + 1 tbsp extra virgin olive oil in a medium frying pan over medium heat. Cook 1 clove crushed garlic + 1 finely chopped fresh long red chilli + 1 tsp finely grated lemon rind + 1 cup coarse sourdough breadcrumbs, stirring, until breadcrumbs are golden and crisp.

SMOKY BRAZIL NUTS & ALMONDS

PREP & COOK TIME 20 MINUTES MAKES 1 CUP

Preheat oven to 180°C/350°F. Place 1 cup coarsely chopped brazil nuts + 1 cup blanched almonds + 1 cup rice puffs on a baking-paper-lined tray. Whisk together 1 egg white + 2 tsp smoked paprika + 1 tsp ground cumin + 1 tsp sea salt flakes with a fork. Toss together spice mixture + nut mixture. Roast for 10 minutes until golden, stirring halfway through cooking time.

CURRY SPRINKLES

PREP & COOK TIME 25 MINUTES (+ STANDING)
MAKES ½ CUP

Stir ¼ cup (20g) shredded coconut + 1 tbsp each sunflower seeds + pepitas (pumpkin seed kernels) + raisins + curry leaves + 2 tsp pure maple syrup + ½ tsp each ground cumin + ground turmeric + ¼ tsp curry powder in a small non-stick frying pan over low heat for 4 minutes until golden.

CHICKPEA CROUTONS

PREP & COOK TIME 20 MINUTES MAKES 1¼ CUPS

Preheat oven to 220°C/425°F. Pat dry a drained and rinsed 400g (12½oz) can chickpeas. Toss with 2 tsp extra virgin olive oil + 1½ tsp each ground cumin and cayenne pepper to coat; spread across a baking-paper-lined tray. Bake for 15 minutes until chickpeas are crisp and golden.

QUINOA PANGRATTATO

PREP & COOK TIME 20 MINUTES MAKES 1⅔ CUPS

Cook ½ cup rinsed white quinoa following packet directions; drain. Heat 2 tbsp oil in a medium frying pan over medium heat. Add quinoa + 2 tbsp each sunflower seeds + coarsely chopped natural almonds + ½ tsp chilli flakes; cook, stirring, for 5 minutes until quinoa browns lightly. Add 2 cloves finely chopped garlic + 2 tbsp chopped flat-leaf parsley; cook, stirring, for 1 minute until fragrant. Transfer to a plate to cool (it will crisp as it cools).

SMOKY MISO BUTTER

PREP & COOK TIME 10 MINUTES (+ COOLING)
MAKES ½ CUP

Melt 25g (¾oz) butter in a small saucepan over low-medium heat. Cook 2 finely chopped shallots, stirring, for 5 minutes until softened. Add ¾ tsp smoked paprika + ¼ tsp dried chilli flakes; cook, stirring, for 30 seconds until fragrant. Add 3 tsp white (shiro) miso; cook, stirring, for a further 30 seconds. Add another 100g (3oz) butter; stir over low heat until just melted and combined. Season. Cool for 10 minutes. Process butter mixture in a small food processor until well combined.

CHICKPEA 'MEATBALL' CACCIATORE

CHICKPEA 'MEATBALLS'

¼ cup (60ml) extra virgin olive oil

1 medium onion (150g), chopped

300g (9½oz) tempeh

400g (12½oz) can chickpeas
(garbanzo beans), drained, rinsed

2 tbsp basil leaves, chopped

¼ cup (20g) freshly grated parmesan

1 egg

CACCIATORE SAUCE

1 tbsp extra virgin olive oil

400g (12½oz) button mushrooms,
sliced

2 cloves garlic, crushed

½ cup (75g) seeded sicilian olives

2 x 400g (12½oz) cans diced tomatoes
with italian herbs

ASSEMBLY INGREDIENTS

150g (4½oz) wholemeal penne,
cooked, drained

¼ cup (20g) freshly grated parmesan

basil leaves, to serve

2 cups (70g) loosely packed
shredded curly kale

1 tsp extra virgin olive oil

1 long bread roll

1 cup (100g) grated mozzarella

200g (6½oz) butternut pumpkin
spaghetti

O MEAL PREP

Chickpea 'meatballs' Heat 2 tbsp oil in a frying pan over medium heat. Cook onion, stirring, for 4 minutes until soft. Process onion + tempeh + chickpeas + basil + parmesan + egg until mixture comes together. Shape tablespoons of mixture into balls. Place on a large tray and drizzle with 1 tbsp oil. Cook under a medium grill for 10 minutes or until golden.

Cacciatore sauce Meanwhile, heat oil in a large saucepan over high heat. Cook mushrooms, stirring, for 4 minutes. Add garlic; cook for 30 seconds. Add olives + tomatoes + 1 cup water; simmer over low heat for 20 minutes until reduced slightly and thickened.

O STORING

Divide chickpea 'meatballs' and cacciatore sauce into 4 portions. Refrigerate for up to 4 days.

O ASSEMBLY (SEE PAGE 150)

Meal 1 Chickpea 'meatball' cacciatore

Meal 2 Chickpea 'meatball' sub

Meal 3 Chickpea cacciatore bowl with pumpkin voodles

Meal 4 Chickpea cacciatore pasta bake

MEAL 1

CHICKPEA 'MEATBALL' CACCIATORE

Reheat 1 portion chickpea 'meatballs' + 1 portion cacciatore sauce. Add half of the hot cooked pasta. Top with grated parmesan + basil leaves.

MEAL 2

CHICKPEA 'MEATBALL' SUB

Reheat 1 portion chickpea 'meatballs' + 1 portion cacciatore sauce. Rub ½ cup (15g) kale leaves with oil. Split bread roll lengthways from the top, without cutting all the way through. Fill roll with kale leaves + chickpea 'meatball' mixture. Top with ½ cup (50g) grated mozzarella and reheat under the grill.

MEAL 3

CHICKPEA CACCIATORE BOWL WITH PUMPKIN VOODLES

Microwave pumpkin spaghetti + 1½ cups (45g) kale on HIGH for 3 minutes. Reheat 1 portion chickpea 'meatballs' + 1 portion cacciatore sauce. Serve hot chickpea 'meatball' mixture with pumpkin spaghetti + kale.

MEAL 4

CHICKPEA CACCIATORE PASTA BAKE

Preheat oven to 200°C/400°F. Place remaining hot cooked pasta + 1 portion chickpea 'meatballs' + 1 portion cacciatore sauce in a shallow 2-cup ovenproof dish; scatter with ½ cup grated mozzarella. Bake for 5 minutes until golden and bubbling. Top with basil leaves.

BUTTER CAULIFLOWER
WITH DHAL GREENS

BUTTER CAULIFLOWER

300g (9½oz) silken tofu

100g (3oz) tomato paste

2 tsp smoked paprika

1 tsp ground turmeric

1 small cauliflower (1kg),
cut into florets

2 tbsp ghee (clarified butter)

1 cup (250ml) vegetable stock

DHAL GREENS

2 tbsp ghee (clarified butter)

2 tsp cumin seeds

400g (12½oz) can brown lentils,
drained, rinsed

½ bunch kale (125g),
stems removed, chopped

160g (5oz) baby spinach leaves

ASSEMBLY INGREDIENTS

2 naan breads (250g)

¼ cup coriander (cilantro) leaves

½ cup (100g) tri-coloured quinoa,
cooked

⅓ cup (80ml) vegetable stock

⅔ cup (190g) greek yoghurt

1 fresh long red chilli

1½ tbsp ghee (clarified butter)

1 egg

⭘ **MEAL PREP**

Butter cauliflower Process tofu + tomato paste + paprika + turmeric until smooth. Cook cauliflower in ghee in a large heavy-based saucepan over high heat, stirring, for 5 minutes until golden. Add tofu mixture + stock; cook for 8 minutes. Season.

Dhal greens Heat ghee in a large frying pan over medium heat; cook cumin for 30 seconds. Add lentils; cook for 3 minutes until warmed through. Add kale; cook for 1 minute. Add spinach; stir until wilted. Season.

⭘ **STORING**

Divide butter cauliflower and dhal greens, separately, into 4 portions. Refrigerate for up to 4 days.

⭘ **ASSEMBLY (SEE PAGE 154)**

Meal 1 Butter cauliflower with dhal greens

Meal 2 Butter cauliflower with dhal quinoa

Meal 3 Butter cauliflower with chilli naan crisps

Meal 4 Butter cauliflower with chilli-fried egg

MEAL 1

BUTTER CAULIFLOWER WITH DHAL GREENS

Serve 1 portion reheated butter cauliflower + 1 portion reheated dhal greens + 1 heated naan bread. Top with 1 tbsp coriander leaves.

MEAL 2

BUTTER CAULIFLOWER WITH DHAL QUINOA

Stir 1 portion dhal greens + half the cooked quinoa + stock in a saucepan over medium heat for 10 minutes until thickened. Stir in 1 portion butter cauliflower until warmed through; mash coarsely. Top with ⅓ cup yoghurt + 1 tbsp coriander leaves.

MEAL 3

BUTTER CAULIFLOWER WITH CHILLI NAAN CRISPS

Tear 1 naan coarsely; toss with ½ chilli, chopped + 1 tbsp ghee. Bake on a baking-paper-lined tray for 8 minutes until golden and crisp. Serve with 1 portion reheated butter cauliflower + 1 portion reheated dhal greens. Top with ⅓ cup yoghurt + 1 tbsp coriander leaves.

MEAL 4

BUTTER CAULIFLOWER WITH CHILLI-FRIED EGG

Cook ½ chilli, sliced, in 2 tsp ghee in a small non-stick frying pan for 1 minute. Add egg; fry until crisp edges form. Serve 1 portion reheated butter cauliflower + 1 portion reheated dhal greens + remaining cooked quinoa + fried egg and chilli. Top with 1 tbsp coriander leaves.

INSTANT
DINNERS

FROM THE FREEZER

ROAST CHICKEN
WITH GREEN PUMPKIN & BROCCOLINI CURRY

ROAST CHICKEN

1 tbsp extra virgin olive oil

1.2kg (2½lb) chicken, patted dry, butterflied

GREEN PUMPKIN & BROCCOLINI CURRY

1 tbsp extra virgin olive oil

2 red shallots, sliced thinly

¼ cup (75g) green curry paste

500g (1lb) butternut pumpkin, peeled, cut into 3cm (1¼in) pieces

400ml can coconut cream

2 bunches broccolini (350g), trimmed, halved crossways

1 tbsp brown sugar

2 tbsp lime juice

SESAME CAULIFLOWER RICE

1 medium cauliflower (1.5kg), cut into florets

1 tbsp sesame oil

3 green onions (scallions), sliced thinly

ASSEMBLY INGREDIENT

thai basil leaves, to serve

⭘ MEAL PREP

Roast chicken Preheat oven to 180°C/350°F. Line an oven tray with baking paper. Rub oil over chicken; season well. Place chicken on lined tray; roast for 50 minutes or until juices run clear. Cover loosely with foil. Rest for 15 minutes before carving.

Green pumpkin & broccolini curry Meanwhile, heat oil in a large heavy-based saucepan over medium heat. Cook shallots, stirring, for 2 minutes. Stir in curry paste; cook for 1 minute. Add pumpkin; stir to coat. Add coconut cream + 1 cup water; bring to the boil. Simmer for 6 minutes. Add broccolini; cook for 3 minutes or until tender but still crisp. Remove broccolini. Stir in sugar + lime juice.

Sesame cauliflower rice Meanwhile, process cauliflower until very finely chopped. Heat sesame oil in a large deep frying pan over medium-high heat. Cook processed cauliflower, stirring, for 12 minutes. Add green onions; cook, stirring, for 3 minutes or until cauliflower is cooked.

⭘ ASSEMBLY

Cut chicken into quarters and serve with pumpkin & broccolini curry + sesame cauliflower rice. Top with thai basil leaves to serve.

⭘ TO FREEZE

Cut chicken into quarters. Divide chicken + pumpkin & broccolini curry + sesame cauliflower rice into 4 individual portions and store in freezer-proof, microwave-safe containers. Label and freeze.

To reheat Thaw in fridge or microwave on DEFROST for 10 minutes. Heat on HIGH for 3 minutes or until chicken is warmed through.

Tip Use purchased frozen cauliflower rice, if preferred.

PORK & GREEN OLIVE MEATLOAVES
WITH SWEET POTATO MASH

PORK & GREEN OLIVE MEATLOAVES

2 tbsp extra virgin olive oil

1 large onion (200g), chopped finely

3 slices sourdough bread (150g), chopped coarsely

¼ cup (60ml) almond milk

500g (1lb) lean minced (ground) pork

1 egg, beaten lightly

1 cup (180g) pitted green sicilian olives, chopped finely

½ cup firmly packed oregano leaves, chopped finely

¼ cup (20g) flaked almonds

250g (8oz) cherry truss tomatoes

SWEET POTATO MASH & BEANS

2 medium orange sweet potatoes (800g), diced

¼ cup (60ml) almond milk

200g (6½oz) trimmed green beans, boiled, steamed or microwaved

O MEAL PREP

Pork & green olive meatloaves Preheat oven to 220°C/425°F. Heat 1 tbsp oil in a large non-stick frying pan over medium heat. Cook onion, stirring, for 6 minutes or until softened; season well. Transfer to a large bowl; cool slightly. Meanwhile, process sourdough until chopped coarsely. Add 1 cup breadcrumbs + almond milk to onion; combine well. Add pork + egg + olives + ¼ cup oregano; mix well. Divide into quarters. Lightly grease four holes of a texas muffin pan and place on an oven tray; press pork mixture into greased holes.

Combine remaining breadcrumbs + ¼ cup oregano + 1 tbsp oil + almonds; season well. Press breadcrumb mixture gently onto meatloaves. Bake for 15 minutes. Remove meatloaves carefully from muffin pan using a pallete knife and place directly on oven tray. Add tomatoes to tray; bake for a further 5 minutes.

Sweet potato mash & beans Meanwhile, boil, steam or microwave sweet potato until tender; drain. Mash potato + almond milk; season.

Boil, steam or microwave beans until tender but still crisp; drain.

O ASSEMBLY

Serve meatloaves + roast tomatoes + sweet potato mash + beans.

O TO FREEZE

Wrap each meatloaf + a quarter of the tomatoes in a 30cm (12in) square foil piece. Divide sweet potato mash & beans into 4 individual portions and store in freezer-proof, microwave-safe containers. Label and freeze.

To reheat Thaw meatloaves + mash & beans in fridge. Preheat oven to 220°C/425°F. Place foil parcels on an oven tray and heat for 10 minutes. Unwrap and heat for a further 5 minutes or until crumb topping is crunchy. Microwave mash & beans on HIGH for 3 minutes.

CHEESY CHICKEN & BEAN BURRITOS

CHEESY CHICKEN & BEAN BURRITOS

300g (9½oz) chicken tenderloins

20g (¾oz) burrito spice mix

1 tbsp extra virgin olive oil

400g (12½oz) can red kidney beans, drained, rinsed

4 green onions (scallions), sliced thinly

12 regular wholegrain tortillas

2 cups (240g) coarsely grated cheddar

250g (8oz) red grape tomatoes, sliced

1 cup loosely packed coriander (cilantro) leaves

olive oil cooking spray

JALAPEÑO YOGHURT

1½ cups (420g) greek yoghurt

60g (2oz) sliced pickled jalapeños, chopped coarsely

O MEAL PREP

Cheesy chicken & bean burritos Combine chicken + burrito spice mix. Heat oil in large non-stick frying pan over medium-high heat. Cook chicken for 3 minutes each side until cooked through. Transfer to a plate; shred. Combine beans + green onions + shredded chicken in a large bowl; season.

Lay a tortilla down on a clean surface; top with 2 tbsp cheddar. Spread ½ cup chicken mixture on bottom third of tortilla. Add 20g (½oz) tomatoes + 1 tbsp coriander leaves. Roll tightly to enclose filling, tucking in ends as you go. Repeat with remaining tortillas, cheddar, chicken mixture and tomatoes to make 12 burritos in total. Spray burritos with oil; toast in a hot sandwich press for 7 minutes or until golden brown and warmed through.

Jalapeño yoghurt Combine yoghurt + jalapeño.

O ASSEMBLY

Serve burritos with jalapeño yoghurt.

O TO FREEZE

Wrap untoasted burritos individually in foil; place two each in resealable plastic bags. Label and freeze.

Jalapeño yoghurt is not suitable to freeze.

To reheat Thaw burritos in the fridge. Place burritos in their foil onto a hot a sandwich press; toast for 12 minutes until golden and warmed through.

SWEET POTATO, CHORIZO & BLACK BEAN CHILLI

SWEET POTATO, CHORIZO & BLACK BEAN CHILLI

1 tbsp extra virgin olive oil

2 cured chorizo sausages (340g), sliced

1 large onion (200g), sliced

1 large orange sweet potato (500g), chopped coarsely

2 cloves garlic, crushed

2 tsp ground cumin

2 tbsp chipotle in adobo sauce, chopped coarsely

2 x 400g (12½oz) cans diced tomatoes

2 x 400g (12½oz) cans black beans, drained, rinsed

ASSEMBLY INGREDIENTS

2 x 250g (8oz) packets microwave brown and red rice blend (see tip)

2 lebanese cucumbers (260g), cut into ribbons

coriander (cilantro) leaves, to serve

lime wedges, to serve

O MEAL PREP

Sweet potato, chorizo & black bean chilli Heat oil in a heavy-based saucepan over medium-high heat. Cook chorizo for 5 minutes until browned; transfer to a plate. Add onion + sweet potato + garlic + cumin + chipotle; cook, stirring, for 1 minute. Stir in tomatoes + 1 cup water. Reduce heat to low; cover and cook for 10 minutes until sweet potato starts to soften. Stir in beans + chorizo; cook for 5 minutes until beans warm through.

O ASSEMBLY

Serve chilli with heated rice + cucumber. Top with coriander leaves. Serve with lime wedges.

O TO FREEZE

Divide chilli into 6 individual portions and store in freezer-proof, microwave-safe containers. Label and freeze.

To reheat Thaw in fridge or microwave on DEFROST for 10–12 minutes. Heat on HIGH for 3 minutes or until chilli is warmed through.

Tip If not serving all of the chilli at once, heat just 1 packet of rice.

HARISSA BEEF, TOMATO & LENTIL STEW

HARISSA BEEF, TOMATO & LENTIL STEW

2 tbsp extra virgin olive oil

800g (1½lb) beef chuck steak, cut into 3cm (1¼in) pieces

1 large onion (200g), chopped coarsely

2 cloves garlic, chopped coarsely

2 tbsp tomato paste

1½ tbsp harissa paste

1 fresh bay leaf

1 litre (4 cups) salt-reduced beef stock

2 x 400g (12½oz) cans cherry tomatoes

2 x 400g (12½oz) cans chickpeas (garbanzo beans), drained, rinsed

400g (12½oz) can brown lentils, drained, rinsed

ASSEMBLY INGREDIENTS

600g (1¼lb) green beans, trimmed, boiled, steamed or microwaved

greek yoghurt, to serve

mint leaves, to serve

⭘ MEAL PREP

Harissa beef, tomato & lentil stew Heat 1 tbsp oil in a large cast iron casserole dish over medium-high heat. Brown beef in batches for 4 minutes, stirring occasionally. Transfer to a plate or bowl. Add another 1 tbsp oil to pan. Cook onion + garlic, stirring, for 3 minutes. Return beef to pan. Add pastes + bay leaf; cook, stirring, for 1 minute. Add stock + tomatoes; bring to the boil. Season. Reduce heat to low; cook, covered, for 1½ hours. Stir in chickpeas + lentils. Cook, uncovered, over medium heat for a further 20 minutes until beef is tender and sauce thickens slightly.

⭘ ASSEMBLY

Serve stew with beans + yoghurt. Top with mint leaves.

⭘ TO FREEZE

Divide stew into 6 individual portions and store in freezer-proof, microwave-safe containers. Label and freeze.

To reheat Thaw in fridge or microwave on DEFROST for 10–15 minutes. Heat on HIGH for 3 minutes or until stew is warmed through.

VIETNAMESE CARAMEL CHILLI PORK

VIETNAMESE CARAMEL CHILLI PORK

1 cup (150g) coconut sugar

4 cloves garlic, sliced thinly

2 fresh long red chillies, sliced thinly

¼ cup (60ml) soy sauce

2 tbsp fish sauce

800g (1½lb) pork tenderloin, trimmed, sliced thinly

BROCCOLINI & NOODLES

2 bunches broccolini (350g), trimmed, halved crossways

200g (6½oz) thin egg noodles

ASSEMBLY INGREDIENTS

2 tbsp coarsely chopped roasted unsalted peanuts

1 fresh red chilli, sliced

⅓ cup coriander (cilantro) leaves

O MEAL PREP

Vietnamese caramel chilli pork Place sugar + ¼ cup water in a large non-stick frying pan over medium heat. Cook, without stirring, for 2 minutes until sugar dissolves. Increase heat to high; cook for 3 minutes, swirling pan occasionally, until a bubbling caramel forms. Carefully add ⅓ cup water + garlic + chilli + soy sauce + fish sauce; bring to a simmer. Cook for 6 minutes or until thickened and sticky. Add pork; cook, turning, for 3 minutes until just cooked through and sauce is sticky.

Broccolini & noodles Meanwhile, cook broccolini in a saucepan of salted boiling water for 3 minutes. Drain; refresh in cold water, then drain again.

Cook egg noodles following packet directions; drain.

O ASSEMBLY

Serve pork + broccolini + noodles, topped with peanuts + chilli + coriander leaves.

O TO FREEZE

Divide pork + noodles + broccolini into 4 individual portions and store in freezer-proof, microwave-safe containers; spoon over caramel sauce. Label and freeze.

To reheat Thaw in fridge or microwave on DEFROST for 8 minutes. Heat on HIGH for 4 minutes or until pork is warmed through.

BASICS

QUINOA

PREP & COOK TIME 20 MINUTES
MAKES 4 PORTIONS

Rinse 1 cup white, red or tri-coloured quinoa in a sieve under cold running water. Place quinoa + 2 cups water in a medium saucepan; bring to the boil. Reduce heat to low; cook, covered, for 15 minutes until quinoa is tender and water is absorbed. Cool slightly.

RICE

PREP & COOK TIME 20 MINUTES FOR WHITE, 30 MINUTES FOR BROWN (+ STANDING)
MAKES 4 PORTIONS

Rinse 1½ cups white or brown rice in a sieve under cold running water until water runs clear. Place 2¼ cups water for white rice or 3 cups for brown rice + ½ tsp salt in a medium saucepan; bring to the boil. Cover; reduce heat to low. Cook white rice for 15 minutes and brown rice for 25 minutes until water is absorbed. Remove pan from heat; stand, covered, for 10 minutes. Fluff rice with a fork.

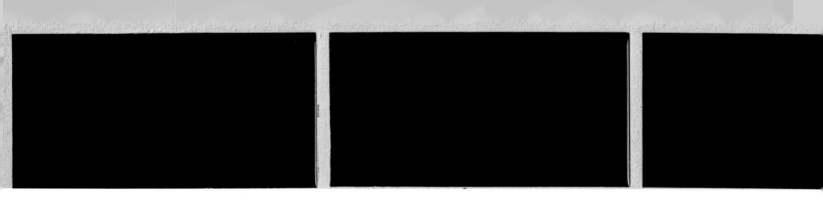

CAULIFLOWER RICE

PREP & COOK TIME 15 MINUTES
MAKES 4 PORTIONS

Coarsely chop 750g (1½lb) cauliflower and stems. Process cauliflower using pulse button until resembling rice grains. Heat 2 tbsp olive oil in a wok over medium heat. Add 2 crushed cloves garlic + 2 tsp finely grated fresh ginger (optional); stir for 1 minute or until fragrant. Add chopped cauliflower; stir occasionally for 4 minutes until softened. Season to taste.

BROCCOLI RICE

PREP & COOK TIME 10 MINUTES
MAKES 4 PORTIONS

Coarsely chop 750g (1½lb) broccoli and stems. Process broccoli using pulse button until resembling rice grains. Heat 2 tbsp olive oil in a wok or large frying pan over medium heat. Add 2 crushed cloves garlic + 2 tsp grated fresh ginger (optional) + 1 finely chopped fresh small red chilli; stir for 1 minute or until fragrant. Add chopped broccoli; stir occasionally for 4 minutes until softened. Season to taste.

MUSHROOM & KALE LASAGNE

KALE BÉCHAMEL SAUCE

60g (2oz) butter

⅓ cup (50g) plain (all-purpose) flour

1 litre (4 cups) milk, warmed

½ bunch kale (250g), stems removed, leaves shredded

½ tsp ground nutmeg

1 cup (80g) grated parmesan

MUSHROOM & KALE LASAGNE

2 tbsp extra virgin olive oil

800g (1½lb) swiss brown mushrooms, sliced

1 medium onion (150g), chopped finely

2 cloves garlic, chopped finely

1 tbsp thyme leaves

250g (8oz) fresh lasagne sheets

225g (7oz) bocconcini, sliced thinly

½ cup (40g) grated parmesan

ASSEMBLY INGREDIENT

60g (2oz) salad leaves

O MEAL PREP

Kale béchamel sauce Heat butter in a heavy-based saucepan over medium heat until melted and starting to bubble. Add flour; cook, stirring continuously, for 4 minutes until a pale straw colour. Remove pan from heat. Add half the milk, whisking until smooth. Add remaining milk, whisking until smooth. Return to heat, stirring, for 5 minutes until thickened. Stir through kale + nutmeg until kale wilts. Stir in parmesan to combine; season.

Mushroom & kale lasagne Preheat oven to 180°C/350°F. Heat oil in a large heavy-based frying pan over medium heat. Cook mushrooms + onion + garlic, stirring, for 15 minutes until browned and liquid is almost evaporated. Add thyme; season.

Lightly grease base and sides of 2.5-litre (10-cup) ovenproof dish. Spoon a quarter of the béchamel sauce over the base. Cover with 2–3 lasagne sheets. Spread half the mushroom mixture over lasagne sheets. Spread another quarter of the béchamel sauce over mushroom mixture. Top with another layer of lasagne sheets. Repeat layering with béchamel sauce + mushroom mixture + lasagne sheets until you finish with a béchamel layer. Lay bocconcini evenly on top, then sprinkle with parmesan. Cover with foil; bake for 15 minutes. Uncover; bake for a further 20 minutes until lasagne sheets are cooked and top is golden brown.

O ASSEMBLY

Serve lasagne with salad leaves.

O TO FREEZE

Divide lasagne into 6 individual portions and store in freezer-proof, microwave-safe containers. Label and freeze.

To reheat Thaw in fridge or microwave on DEFROST for 10–12 minutes. Heat on HIGH for 3 minutes or until lasagne is warmed through.

MUSTARD & LEMON SALMON TRAY BAKE

LEMON SALMON TRAY BAKE

1 tbsp extra virgin olive oil

500g (1lb) microwave brown rice and quinoa

400g (12½oz) can brown lentils, drained, rinsed

480g (15½oz) baby spinach leaves

1 large lemon, rind grated finely, then juiced

500g (1lb) red sauerkraut, drained

4 x 230g (7oz) skinless boneless salmon fillets

HONEY-MUSTARD DRESSING

1 tbsp chopped dill

1 tbsp dijon mustard

1½ tbsp honey

O MEAL PREP

Lemon salmon tray bake Preheat oven to 220°C/425°F. Heat oil in a large ovenproof frying pan over medium heat. Cook rice + lentils + spinach + 1 tsp lemon rind, stirring occasionally, for 3 minutes until spinach starts to wilt; season well. Add sauerkraut. Place salmon on top of rice mixture; season. Drizzle with 2 tbsp lemon juice. Transfer to oven; bake for 10 minutes until salmon is just cooked.

Honey-mustard dressing Meanwhile, combine dill + mustard + honey; season.

O ASSEMBLY

Serve salmon tray bake drizzled with honey-mustard dressing.

O TO FREEZE

Divide salmon tray bake into 4 individual portions and store in freezer-proof, microwave-safe containers. Divide honey-mustard dressing into 4 individual portions. Label and freeze.

To reheat Thaw in fridge. Microwave salmon tray bake on HIGH for 4 minutes or until salmon is warmed through. Serve with the thawed dressing.

Tip You can freeze the meal before cooking the salmon, if you like. Combine the oil + rice + lentils + spinach + lemon rind. Divide mixture among four freezer-proof, oven-proof containers. Top evenly with the sauerkraut + salmon. Label and freeze. To cook, thaw in fridge. Place ovenproof dish/es on an oven tray and bake for 10 minutes in a preheated 220°C/425°F oven until the salmon is just cooked through. Serve with thawed honey-mustard dressing.

TERIYAKI-SEARED STEAK

WITH SOBA & EDAMAME GREENS

TERIYAKI-SEARED STEAK

½ cup (125ml) teriyaki sauce

2 tbsp sesame oil

⅓ cup (95g) pickled pink ginger, chopped finely

4 x 200g (6½oz) beef scotch fillet steaks

⅓ cup (50g) white sesame seeds

SOBA & EDAMAME GREENS

270g (8½oz) buckwheat soba noodles

300g (9½oz) sugar snap peas, trimmed

1 cup (200g) frozen shelled edamame (soy beans), thawed

1 bunch asparagus (170g), trimmed, halved crossways

ASSEMBLY INGREDIENTS

2 green onions (scallions), sliced thinly

1 fresh long green chilli, sliced thinly (optional)

⭕ MEAL PREP

Teriyaki-seared steak Combine teriyaki sauce + 1½ tbsp sesame oil + pickled ginger in a shallow bowl. Add steaks; turn to coat. Season well. Leave at room temperature for 15 minutes. Heat a large non-stick frying pan over high heat. Remove steaks from marinade and pat dry; press into sesame seeds. Add remaining 2 tsp sesame oil to pan; cook steaks for 4 minutes each side until golden and cooked to medium-rare. Remove from pan. Cover loosely with foil and rest for 5 minutes.

To make the sauce, reduce heat to low; cook marinade + ⅓ cup water, stirring, for 30 seconds or until simmering.

Soba & edamame greens Meanwhile, cook soba noodles in a saucepan of salted boiling water following packet directions. Add sugar snap peas + edamame + asparagus for last 1 minute of cooking time; drain. Rinse under cold running water; drain.

⭕ ASSEMBLY

Slice steaks thickly on the diagonal. Serve with soba & edamame greens + green onions + chilli.

⭕ TO FREEZE

Divide the soba & edamame greens + sliced teriyaki-seared steak into 4 individual portions and store in freezer-proof, microwave-safe containers with two compartments; put the greens and steak in one compartment and the sauce in the other compartment. Label and freeze.

To reheat Thaw in fridge or microwave on DEFROST for 6 minutes. Heat on HIGH for 3 minutes or until steak is warmed through.

LAMB & APRICOT 'TAGINE' TRAY BAKE

LAMB & APRICOT 'TAGINE' TRAY BAKE

1 tbsp extra virgin olive oil

12 lamb loin chops (1.2kg)

1 onion (150g), halved, sliced

2 cloves garlic, crushed

2 tsp finely grated fresh ginger

2 tbsp harissa spice mix

1 cup (250ml) chicken stock

1 cup (250ml) apricot nectar

1 medium parsnip (250g), chopped coarsely

1 bunch baby carrots (400g), trimmed, scrubbed

½ cup (75g) dried apricots

ZUCCHINI ZOODLES

5 medium zucchini (600g), spiralised (see page 182)

ASSEMBLY INGREDIENT

flat-leaf parsley leaves, to serve

○ MEAL PREP

Lamb & apricot 'tagine' tray bake Preheat oven to 180°C/350°F. Heat oil in a large flameproof non-stick roasting pan over high heat. Cook chops in two batches for 1 minute each side. Transfer to a plate. Reduce heat to medium; cook onion, stirring occasionally, for 5 minutes until softened. Add garlic + ginger + harissa; cook for 1 minute until aromatic. Add stock + nectar; bring to the boil. Add parsnip + carrots. Cover tightly with foil; bake for 15 minutes. Remove foil; add apricots and chops. Stir to coat. Re-cover with foil; bake for a further 10 minutes or until chops and vegetables are cooked through.

Zucchini zoodles Meanwhile, steam zucchini zoodles in a large bowl in microwave on HIGH for 1½ minutes or until just softened.

○ ASSEMBLY

Serve lamb tray bake + zucchini zoodles scattered with parsley leaves.

○ TO FREEZE

Divide lamb tray bake + zucchini zoodles into 6 individual portions and store in freezer-proof, microwave-safe containers. Label and freeze.

To reheat Thaw in fridge or microwave on DEFROST for 10 minutes. Heat on HIGH for 3 minutes or until lamb is warmed through.

PUTTANESCA FISH PARCELS

WITH SUPER-GREEN SALSA VERDE

PUTTANESCA FISH PARCELS

1 tbsp extra virgin olive oil

3 cloves garlic, sliced thinly

1 tbsp capers

1 cup (240g) marinated antipasti vegetables, chopped

400g (12½oz) can cherry tomatoes

180g (5½oz) wholemeal spaghetti

300g (9½oz) green beans, trimmed

4 x 200g (6½oz) skinless boneless blue eye trevalla fillets

1 tbsp lemon juice

SALSA VERDE

2 cups (70g) loosely packed shredded curly kale

1 cup firmly packed flat-leaf parsley leaves

¼ cup (60ml) extra virgin olive oil

1 clove garlic, crushed

1 tbsp capers

1 tsp finely grated lemon rind

2 tbsp lemon juice

O MEAL PREP

Puttanesca fish parcels Preheat oven to 220°C/425°F. To make puttanesca sauce, heat oil in a medium non-stick frying pan over medium heat. Cook garlic + capers + antipasti vegetables, stirring, for 4 minutes until mixture is fragrant. Add tomatoes; season. Simmer for 6 minutes until sauce is reduced; remove from heat.

Meanwhile, cook spaghetti in a large saucepan of salted boiling water for 6 minutes until just tender; add beans in the last 30 seconds of cooking time. Drain. Rinse under cold running water; drain.

Divide spaghetti + beans among four 30cm (12in) baking-paper squares. Top with fish + puttanesca sauce + lemon juice; season well. Fold ends and sides of paper over to enclose fish (secure parcel with kitchen string, if necessary). Wrap in foil. Bake fish parcels on an oven tray for 25 minutes until fish is cooked. Stand for 5 minutes.

Salsa verde Meanwhile, steam, boil or microwave kale until just tender. Refresh in cold water; drain. Process kale + parsley + oil + garlic + capers + lemon rind + lemon juice until finely chopped and combined; season well.

O ASSEMBLY

Serve fish parcels + salsa verde.

O TO FREEZE

Label and freeze fish parcels + individual portions of salsa verde.

To reheat Thaw fish parcels and salsa verde in fridge. Bake thawed fish parcels following cooking directions above. Serve with thawed salsa verde.

BASICS

VOODLES

A spiraliser is a gadget that cuts vegetables to resemble noodles. If you don't have one, you can use a julienne peeler or a julienne attachment on a mandoline or V-slicer.

There are various cooking methods for vegetable noodles (voodles):

Blanching Add voodles to a large pot of boiling salted water; boil for 1 minute until just tender. Drain well. Cooking time will vary depending on the type of vegetable being used.

Pan-frying Heat some oil or butter in a large frying pan over medium heat; add voodles and cook for 1 minute or until just tender. Cooking time will vary depending on the type of vegetable being used.

Raw Raw voodles are a great addition to any salad, tossed gently in a tangy citrus dressing.

MASH

PREP & COOK TIME 30 MINUTES
MAKES 4 PORTIONS

Peel and coarsely chop either 1kg (2lb) coliban, toolangi delight, king edward or dutch cream potatoes. Place potatoes in a medium saucepan with cold water to just cover them. Boil over medium heat for 15 minutes or until tender; drain. Return potato to pan and mash until smooth (or use a potato ricer or mouli). Add 40g (1½oz) butter and ¾ cup (180ml) hot milk; fold in gently until mash is smooth. Season to taste.

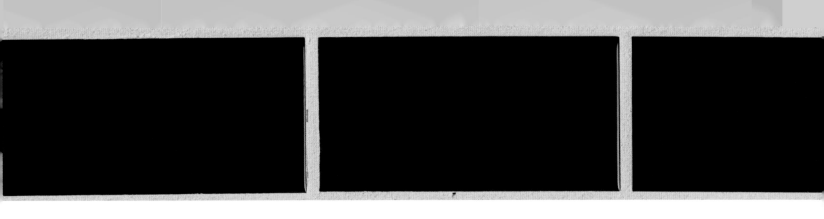

BOILED EGGS

PREP & COOK TIME 10 MINUTES MAKES 4

Place 4 room temperature eggs in a small pan with cold water to just cover eggs. Cover; bring water to the boil over high heat. Remove the lid; boil eggs until yolks are as soft or as firm as you like (3 mins for soft-boiled, 4 mins for medium-boiled and 5 mins for hard-boiled). Remove eggs from water. For medium- or hard-boiled eggs, cool under cold running water. Roll eggs on a work surface to crack the shell, then peel.

Tip To centralise the yolk, which looks best if you are halving boiled eggs to put in a salad, stir the eggs continuously with a wooden spoon over high heat until the water boils.

POACHED EGGS

PREP & COOK TIME 5 MINUTES MAKES 4

Half-fill a large shallow frying pan with water and add 2 tsp vinegar; bring to the boil. Using 4 eggs, break 1 egg at a time into a small bowl or cup. Swirl boiling water with a whisk to create a whirlpool, then slide the egg into the pan. Repeat with remaining eggs. Allow the water to return to boil. Cover pan and turn off the heat. Stand for 4 minutes or until a light film of egg white sets over the yolks. Remove eggs with a slotted spoon; drain on paper towel.

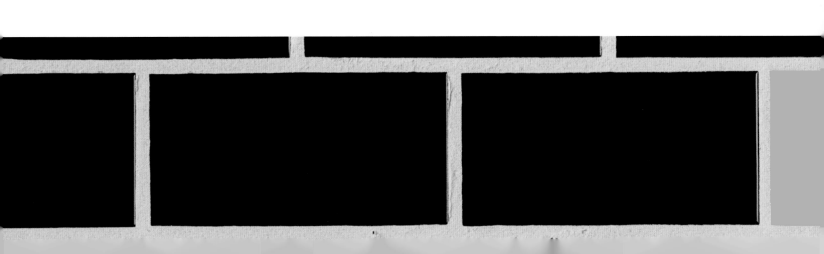

PREP & COOK TIME | MAKES
25 MINUTES | 4 PORTIONS

SMOKY LAMB KOFTAS
WITH EAT-YOUR-GREENS SMASH

SMOKY LAMB KOFTAS

2 tbsp extra virgin olive oil

1 large onion (200g), chopped finely

2 tsp smoked paprika

½ cup (40g) panko (japanese) breadcrumbs

¼ cup firmly packed flat-leaf parsley leaves, chopped finely

500g (1lb) minced (ground) lamb

400g (12½oz) bottle arrabbiata pasta sauce

285g (9oz) piquillo peppers, drained

EAT-YOUR-GREENS SMASH & BROCCOLI

2 tbsp extra virgin olive oil

3 x 400g (12½oz) cans cannellini beans, drained, rinsed

1 small lemon, rind grated

3 cups (135g) firmly packed thinly sliced silverbeet (swiss chard)

2 green onions (scalllions), sliced thinly

1 large head broccoli (400g), cut into florets

⭘ MEAL PREP

Smoky lamb koftas Heat 1 tbsp oil in a large ovenproof frying pan over medium heat. Cook onion + paprika, stirring, for 6 minutes until onion softens; season well. Mix onion mixture with breadcrumbs + parsley + lamb; season. Combine well. Roll tablespoons of mixture into balls. Wipe pan. Heat 1 tbsp oil in pan over medium-high heat; cook meatballs, turning, for 3 minutes until browned. Add pasta sauce + ¾ cup water + piquillo peppers; season well. Reduce heat to low; cook for a further 9 minutes untill koftas are cooked through and sauce thickens slightly.

Eat-your-greens smash & broccoli Meanwhile, cook oil + beans + lemon rind + ¾ cup water in a medium saucepan over medium heat, stirring, for 5 minutes until warmed through. Crush coarsely using a potato masher or fork. Add silverbeet + green onions; cook, stirring, for 1 minute until silverbeet is tender. Season.

Steam, boil or microwave broccoli until tender but still crisp.

⭘ ASSEMBLY

Serve lamb koftas + eat-your-greens smash + broccoli.

⭘ TO FREEZE

Divide lamb koftas + greens smash + broccoli into 4 individual portions and store in freezer-proof microwave-safe containers. Label and freeze.

To reheat Thaw in fridge or microwave on DEFROST for 6 minutes. Heat on HIGH for 4 minutes or until koftas are warmed through.

PUMPKIN, CHICKPEA & PANEER TIKKA TRAY BAKE

PUMPKIN, CHICKPEA & PANEER TIKKA TRAY BAKE

400g (12½oz) can diced tomatoes

400g (12½oz) can chickpeas (garbanzo beans), drained, rinsed

400ml can coconut milk

¼ cup (75g) tikka masala paste

850g (1¾lb) kent pumpkin, seeded, cut into wedges

olive oil cooking spray

200g (6½oz) paneer cheese, cut into 12 pieces

COCONUT SPRINKLE

⅓ cup (15g) flaked coconut, toasted

¼ cup (50g) pepitas (pumpkin seed kernels), chopped coarsely

1 tsp finely grated lime rind

ASSEMBLY INGREDIENTS

500g (1lb) microwave white rice, heated

○ MEAL PREP

Pumpkin, chickpea & paneer tikka tray bake Preheat oven to 220°C/425°F. Combine tomatoes + chickpeas + coconut milk + ½ cup water + tikka paste in a large deep roasting pan. Add pumpkin; spray lightly with oil. Season well. Cover with foil; bake for 20 minutes. Uncover; add paneer and bake for a further 15 minutes until pumpkin is tender and golden.

Coconut sprinkle Meanwhile, combine coconut + pepitas + lime rind.

○ ASSEMBLY

Serve tikka tray bake + heated rice topped with coconut sprinkle.

○ TO FREEZE

Divide tikka tray bake + rice into 4 individual portions and store in freezer-proof, microwave-safe containers. Divide coconut sprinkle among four sheets of baking paper and wrap up tightly. Label and freeze.

To reheat Thaw tikka tray bake in fridge. Microwave on HIGH for 6 minutes until pumpkin is warmed through. Thaw coconut sprinkle at room temperature just before serving.

LIME PICKLE ROAST CHICKEN

WITH CHEAT'S PILAF

LIME PICKLE ROAST CHICKEN

2 tbsp (40g) lime pickle, chopped finely

½ cup (140g) coconut yoghurt

1 tbsp honey

1kg (2lb) chicken thigh fillets, cut into 5cm (2in) pieces

CHEAT'S PILAF & PEAS

2 tbsp extra virgin olive oil

2 medium onions (300g), sliced thinly

1 stick cinnamon

½ cup (140g) coconut yoghurt

500g (1lb) microwave coconut basmati rice

1 tsp garam masala

2 cups (240g) frozen peas

○ MEAL PREP

Lime pickle roast chicken Preheat oven to 220°C/425°F. Combine lime pickle + yoghurt + honey + ½ cup water in a large bowl. Add chicken and toss to coat; season well. Cover bowl; refrigerate for 15 minutes. Place chicken on a lightly greased oven tray; season. Roast for 15 minutes until golden.

Cheat's pilaf & peas Meanwhile, heat 1 tbsp oil in a large non-stick frying pan over medium heat. Cook onion + cinnamon, stirring, for 8 minutes until onion is golden. Remove half the onion and reserve. Stir in yoghurt + 1 cup water. Stir in rice + garam marsala; season. Cover; cook for 5 minutes until liquid is absorbed.

Blanch peas in a saucepan of boiling water for 1 minute; drain. Toss together peas + reserved onion; season.

○ ASSEMBLY

Serve lime pickle roast chicken + peas + cheat's pilaf.

○ TO FREEZE

Divide lime pickle roast chicken + cheat's pilaf + peas into 4 individual portions and store in freezer-proof, microwave-safe containers. Label and freeze.

To reheat Thaw in fridge. Microwave on HIGH for 6 minutes or until chicken is warmed through.

MOROCCAN PULLED BEEF

MOROCCAN PULLED BEEF

1 bunch coriander (cilantro)

2 tbsp olive oil

1.5kg (3lb) piece beef bolar blade roast

2 tbsp moroccan seasoning

1 onion (150g), chopped finely

2 cloves garlic, crushed

1 tbsp harissa paste

1 tbsp ground cumin

1 litre (4 cups) beef stock

400g (12½oz) can cherry tomatoes

TAHINI DRIZZLE

⅓ cup (90g) tahini

¼ cup (60ml) lemon juice

½ tsp ground cumin

ASSEMBLY INGREDIENTS

basic couscous or basic quinoa (see page 170), to serve

○ MEAL PREP

Moroccan pulled beef Preheat oven to 160°C/325°F. Separate coriander leaves from stems and roots (reserve leaves for serving). Wash stems and roots well; chop finely. Heat oil in a 5.75-litre (23-cup) cast iron or other flameproof casserole dish. Coat beef in moroccan seasoning. Cook for 3 minutes each side until browned; transfer beef to a plate. Reduce heat to low. Add onion; cook, stirring, for 5 minutes until softened. Add garlic + harissa + cumin + chopped coriander stems and roots; cook, stirring, for 30 seconds until fragrant. Add stock + tomatoes + beef; season. Cover; bake in oven for 3 hours until beef is very tender.

Tahini drizzle Meanwhile, whisk tahini + lemon juice + cumin + ¼ cup water in a small bowl until smooth; season.

○ ASSEMBLY

Shred beef using two forks. Serve pulled beef + tahini drizzle + couscous or quinoa. Top with reserved coriander leaves, if you like.

○ TO FREEZE

Divide pulled beef into 8 portions and store in freezer-proof, microwave-safe containers. Label and freeze. Freeze individual portions of tahini drizzle.

To reheat Thaw pulled beef and tahini drizzle in fridge. Microwave beef on HIGH for 3 minutes until warmed through. Serve with thawed tahini drizzle.

Tip Omit making the tahini drizzle and instead serve with your favourite purchased hummus with lemon juice swirled through.

GLOSSARY

BEANS

black also called turtle beans or black kidney beans; an earthy-flavoured dried bean completely different from the better-known Chinese black beans (which are fermented soy beans). Used mostly in Mexican and South American cooking.

cannellini small white bean similar in appearance and flavour to other phaseolus vulgaris varieties (great northern, navy or haricot). Available dried or canned.

kidney medium-size red bean, slightly floury in texture yet sweet in flavour; sold dried or canned, it's found in bean mixes and is used in chilli con carne.

BROCCOLINI a cross between broccoli and chinese kale; it has long asparagus-like stems with a long loose floret, both are edible. Resembles broccoli but is milder in taste.

BUK CHOY also known as bok choy, pak choi, chinese white cabbage or chinese chard; has a fresh, mild mustard taste. Use stems and leaves, stir-fried or braised. Baby buk choy, also known as pak kat farang or shanghai bok choy, is smaller and more tender. Its mildly acrid, appealing taste has made it one of the most commonly used asian greens.

CAPERS grey-green buds of a warm climate shrub (usually Mediterranean), sold either dried and salted or pickled in a vinegar brine.

CHEESE

bocconcini from the diminutive of 'boccone', meaning 'mouthful' in Italian; walnut-sized, baby mozzarella, a delicate, semi-soft, white cheese traditionally made from buffalo milk. Sold fresh, it spoils rapidly so will only keep, refrigerated in brine, for 1 or 2 days at the most.

fetta Greek in origin; a crumbly textured goat's or sheep's milk cheese having a sharp, salty taste. Ripened and stored in salted whey; particularly good cubed and tossed into salads.

haloumi a firm, cream-coloured sheep's milk cheese matured in brine; haloumi can be grilled or fried, briefly, without breaking down. Should be eaten while still warm as it becomes rubbery on cooling.

mozzarella soft, spun-curd cheese; originating in Southern Italy where it was traditionally made from water-buffalo milk. Now generally made from cow's milk, it is the most popular pizza cheese because of its low melting point and elasticity when heated.

parmesan also called parmigiano; a hard, grainy cow's milk cheese from the Parma region of Italy. The curd is salted in brine for a month, then aged for up to 2 years.

ricotta a soft, sweet, moist, white cow's milk cheese with a low fat content and a slightly grainy texture. The name roughly translates as 'cooked again' and refers to ricotta's manufacture from a whey that is itself a by-product of other cheese-making.

CHICKPEAS (GARBANZO BEANS) an irregularly round, sandy-coloured legume. Has a firm texture even after cooking, a floury mouth-feel and robust nutty flavour; available canned or dried.

CHIA SEEDS contain protein and all the essential amino acids, as well as being fibre rich and a wealth of vitamins, minerals and antioxidants.

CHILLI

cayenne pepper a long, thin-fleshed, extremely hot red chilli usually sold dried and ground.

chipotle (pronounced cheh-pote-lay) The name used for jalapeño chillies once they've been dried and smoked. They have a deep, intensely smoky flavour, rather than a searing heat, and are dark brown, almost black in colour and wrinkled in appearance.

flakes also sold as crushed chilli; dehydrated deep-red extremely fine slices and whole seeds.

green any unripened chilli; also some particular varieties that are ripe when green, such as jalapeño, habanero, poblano or serrano.

jalapeño (pronounced hah-lah-pain-yo) Fairly hot, medium-sized, plump, dark green chilli; available pickled – sold canned or bottled – and fresh, from greengrocers.

long red available both fresh and dried; a generic term used for any moderately hot, long chilli (about 6cm/2½in to 8cm/3¼in long).

CHORIZO sausage of Spanish origin, made of coarsely ground pork and highly seasoned with garlic and chilli. They are deeply smoked, very spicy. You can buy fresh and dry-cured and both need to be cooked.

COCONUT

cream obtained commercially from the first pressing of the coconut flesh alone, without the addition of water; the second pressing (less rich) is sold as coconut milk. Available in cans and cartons at most supermarkets.

flaked dried flaked coconut flesh.

milk not the liquid found inside the fruit, which is called coconut water, but the diluted liquid from the second pressing of the white flesh of a mature coconut (the first pressing produces coconut cream). Available in cans and cartons at most supermarkets.

sugar (coconut palm sugar) is not made from coconuts, but from the sap of the blossoms of the coconut palm tree. The sap is collected and then boiled to evaporate the water content, leaving a sugar that looks a little like raw or light brown sugar with a similar caramel flavour.

CORIANDER (CILANTRO) a bright-green leafy herb with a pungent flavour. Both stems and roots of coriander are also used in cooking; wash well before using. Also available ground or as seeds; these should not be substituted for fresh as the tastes are completely different.

COUSCOUS a fine, dehydrated, grain-like cereal product made from semolina; it swells to three or four times its original size when liquid is added.

CUMIN resembling caraway in size, cumin is the dried seed of a plant related to the parsley family. Black cumin seeds are smaller than standard cumin, and dark brown rather than true black.

CURRY POWDER a blend of ground spices used for making Indian and some South-East Asian dishes. Consists of some of the following spices: dried chilli, cinnamon, coriander, cumin, fennel, fenugreek, mace, cardamom and turmeric. Available mild or hot.

EDAMAME (SOY BEANS) are fresh soy beans in the pod; available frozen from Asian food stores and supermarkets.

FENNEL also called finocchio or anise; a crunchy green vegetable slightly resembling celery that's eaten raw in salads, fried as an accompaniment, or used as an ingredient in soups and sauces. Also the name given to the dried seeds of the plant which have a stronger licorice flavour.

FISH SAUCE called naam pla on the label if Thai-made, or nuoc naam if Vietnamese; the two are almost identical. Made from pulverised salted fermented fish (most often anchovies); has a pungent smell and strong taste.

GAI LAN also known as gai larn, chinese broccoli and chinese kale; green vegetable appreciated more for its stems than its coarse leaves. Can be served steamed and stir-fried, and in soups and noodle dishes. One of the most popular Asian greens.

GARAM MASALA literally meaning blended spices in its northern Indian place of origin; based on varying proportions of cardamom, cinnamon, cloves, coriander, fennel and cumin, roasted and ground together. Black pepper and chilli can be added for a hotter version.

GINGER

fresh also called green or root ginger; the thick gnarled root of a tropical plant. Can be kept, peeled, covered with dry sherry in a jar and refrigerated, or frozen in an airtight container.

pickled pink or red coloured; available, packaged, from Asian food shops. Pickled paper-thin shavings of ginger in a mixture of vinegar, sugar and natural colouring; used in Japanese cooking.

HARISSA a Moroccan paste made from dried chillies, cumin, garlic, oil and caraway seeds. Available from Middle Eastern food shops and supermarkets.

HUMMUS a Middle Eastern dip made from softened dried chickpeas, garlic, lemon juice and tahini; can be purchased ready-made from most delicatessens and supermarkets. Also the Arabic word for chickpeas.

KAFFIR LIME LEAVES looks like two glossy dark green leaves joined end to end, forming a rounded hourglass shape. Used fresh or dried in many South-East Asian dishes, they are used like bay leaves or curry leaves, especially in Thai cooking. A strip of fresh lime peel may be substituted for each kaffir lime leaf.

KECAP MANIS (pronounced ketjap manis) a thick soy sauce with added sugar and spices. The sweetness is derived from the addition of molasses or palm sugar.

LENTILS (red, brown, yellow) dried pulses often identified by and named after their colour. Eaten by cultures all over the world, most famously perhaps in the dhals of India, lentils have high food value.

LINSEEDS also known as flaxseeds, they are the richest plant source of omega 3 fats, which are essential for a healthy brain, heart, joints and immune system.

MAPLE SYRUP, PURE distilled from the sap of sugar maple trees found only in Canada and the USA. Maple-flavoured syrup or pancake syrup are not adequate substitutes for the real thing.

MIRIN a Japanese champagne-coloured cooking wine, made of glutinous rice and alcohol. It is used expressly for cooking and should not be confused with sake.

MISO fermented soy bean paste. There are many types of miso, each with its own aroma, flavour, colour and texture; it can be kept, airtight, for up to a year in the fridge. Generally, the darker the miso, the saltier the taste and denser the texture. Salt-reduced miso is available.

MUSTARD

dijon also called french. Pale brown, creamy, distinctively flavoured, fairly mild French mustard.

wholegrain also known as seeded. A French-style coarse-grain mustard made from crushed mustard seeds and Dijon-style french mustard. Works well with cold meats and sausages.

NORI a type of dried seaweed used in Japanese cooking as a flavouring, garnish or for sushi. Sold in thin sheets, plain or toasted (yaki-nori).

NUTMEG a strong and pungent spice ground from the dried nut of an evergreen tree native to Indonesia. Usually found ground but the flavour is more intense from a whole nut, so it's best to grate your own.

PANKO BREADCRUMBS also called japanese breadcrumbs. Available in two kinds: larger pieces and fine crumbs; have a lighter texture than Western-style ones. Available from Asian food stores and most major supermarkets.

PAPRIKA ground dried sweet red capsicum (bell pepper); there are many grades and types available, including sweet, hot, mild and smoked.

PEPITAS are the pale green kernels of dried pumpkin seeds; they can be bought plain or salted.

PINE NUTS also known as pignoli; not a nut but a small, cream-coloured kernel from pine cones. They are best roasted before use to bring out the flavour.

POMEGRANATE dark-red, leathery-skinned fresh fruit about the size of an orange filled with hundreds of seeds, each wrapped in an edible lucent-crimson pulp having a unique tangy sweet-sour flavour.

POMEGRANATE MOLASSES not to be confused with pomegranate syrup or grenadine; pomegranate molasses is thicker, browner and more concentrated in flavour – tart, sharp, slightly sweet and fruity.

QUINOA (pronounced keen-wa) is cooked and eaten as a grain alternative but is in fact a seed; has a delicate, nutty taste and chewy texture. Gluten free.

ROCKET also called arugula, rugula and rucola; peppery green leaf eaten raw in salads or used in cooking. Baby rocket leaves are smaller and less peppery.

SESAME SEEDS black and white are the most common of this small oval seed, however there are also red and brown varieties. The seeds are used as an ingredient and as a condiment.

SRIRACHA is a medium-hot chilli sauce available from Asian food stores and some major supermarkets.

SUMAC a purple-red, astringent spice, ground from berries growing on shrubs that flourish wild around the Mediterranean; adds a tart, lemony flavour.

SUNFLOWER SEEDS grey-green, slightly soft, oily kernels; a nutritious snack.

TAHINI a rich, sesame-seed paste.

THAI BASIL also known as horapa; different from holy basil and sweet basil in both look and taste, with smaller leaves and purplish stems. It has a slight aniseed taste and is one of the identifying flavours of Thai food.

TOFU also known as soy bean curd or bean curd; an off-white, custard-like product made from the 'milk' of crushed soy beans. Comes fresh as soft or firm, and processed as fried or pressed dried sheets. Fresh tofu can be refrigerated in water (changed daily) for 4 days.

firm made by compressing bean curd to remove most of the water. Good used in stir-fries as it can be tossed without disintegrating. Can also be flavoured, preserved in rice wine or brine.

silken not a type of tofu but reference to the manufacturing process of straining soy bean liquid through silk; this denotes best quality.

TURMERIC also called kamin; is a rhizome related to galangal and ginger. Must be grated or pounded to release its acrid aroma and pungent flavour. Known for the golden colour it imparts, fresh turmeric can be substituted with the more commonly found dried powder (proportions are 1 teaspoon of ground turmeric for every 20g of fresh turmeric).

ZUCCHINI also known as courgette; belongs to the squash family.

CONVERSION CHART

MEASURES

One Australian metric measuring cup holds approximately 250ml; one Australian metric tablespoon holds 20ml; one Australian metric teaspoon holds 5ml.
The difference between one country's measuring cups and another's is within a two- or three-teaspoon variance and will not affect your cooking results. North America, New Zealand and the United Kingdom use a 15ml tablespoon. All cup and spoon measurements are level.

The most accurate way of measuring dry ingredients is to weigh them.

When measuring liquids, use a clear glass or plastic jug with the metric markings.

We use extra-large eggs with an average weight of 60g.

DRY MEASURES

metric	imperial
15g	½oz
30g	1oz
60g	2oz
90g	3oz
125g	4oz (¼lb)
155g	5oz
185g	6oz
220g	7oz
250g	8oz (½lb)
280g	9oz
315g	10oz
345g	11oz
375g	12oz (¾lb)
410g	13oz
440g	14oz
470g	15oz
500g	16oz (1lb)
750g	24oz (1½lb)
1kg	32oz (2lb)

LIQUID MEASURES

metric	imperial
30ml	1 fluid oz
60ml	2 fluid oz
100ml	3 fluid oz
125ml	4 fluid oz
150ml	5 fluid oz
190ml	6 fluid oz
250ml	8 fluid oz
300ml	10 fluid oz
500ml	16 fluid oz
600ml	20 fluid oz
1000ml (1 litre)	1¾ pints

LENGTH MEASURES

metric	imperial
3mm	⅛in
6mm	¼in
1cm	½in
2cm	¾in
2.5cm	1in
5cm	2in
6cm	2½in
8cm	3in
10cm	4in
13cm	5in
15cm	6in
18cm	7in
20cm	8in
22cm	9in
25cm	10in
28cm	11in
30cm	12in (1ft)

OVEN TEMPERATURES

The oven temperatures in this book are for conventional and fan-forced ovens.

	°C (Celsius)	°F (Fahrenheit)
Very slow	120	250
Slow	150	300
Moderately slow	160	325
Moderate	180	350
Moderately hot	200	400
Hot	220	425
Very hot	240	475

Measurements for cake pans are approximate only. Using same-shaped cake pans of a similar size should not affect the outcome of your baking. We measure the inside top of the cake pan to determine size.

INDEX

Published in 2020 by Bauer Media Books, Australia.
Bauer Media Books is a division of Bauer Media Pty Ltd.

BAUER MEDIA GROUP

Chief executive officer
Brendon Hill

Chief financial officer
Andrew Stedwell

BAUER MEDIA BOOKS

Publisher
Sally Eagle

Editorial & food director
Sophia Young

Creative director
Hannah Blackmore

Managing editor
Stephanie Kistner

Art director & designer
Jeannel Cunanan

Food editors
Kathleen Davis, Sophia Young

Recipe developers
Elizabeth Fiducia, Rebecca Lyall

Senior editor
Chantal Gibbs

Operations manager
David Scotto

Business development manager
Simone Aquilna
saquilina@bauer-media.com.au
Ph +61 2 8268 6278

Photographer
James Moffatt

Stylist
Kate Brown

Photochef
Rebecca Lyall

Printed in China by
1010 Printing International

A catalogue record for this book
is available from the National
Library of Australia.
ISBN 978-1-92586-503-5

© Bauer Media Pty Limited 2020
ABN 18 053 273 546

This publication is copyright.
No part of it may be reproduced
or transmitted in any form
without the written permission
of the publisher.

Published by Bauer Media Books,
a division of Bauer Media Pty Ltd,
54 Park St, Sydney; GPO Box 4088,
Sydney, NSW 2001, Australia
Ph +61 2 8116 9334;
Fax +61 2 9126 3702
www.awwcookbooks.com.au

International rights manager
Simone Aquilina
saquilina@bauer-media.com.au
Ph +61 2 8268 6278

Order books
phone 136 116 (within Australia)
or order online at
www.awwcookbooks.com.au

Send recipe enquiries to
recipeenquiries@bauer-media.com.au

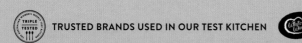

TRUSTED BRANDS USED IN OUR TEST KITCHEN